I Killed Maria Goretti

PIETRO DI DONATO

I KILLED MARIA GORETTI

The Life and Repentance
of Alessandro Serenelli

SOPHIA INSTITUTE PRESS
Manchester, New Hampshire

Copyright © 2025, 1962 by Pietro Di Donato.

Previously published as *The Penitent* © 1962 Hawthorn Books, New York City, NY

Printed in the United States of America. All rights reserved.

Cover by Updatefordesign Studio
Cover image: *Shadow of Disappearing Man* by Westend61 (Adobe Stock 571152547)

No part of this book may be reproduced, stored in a retrieval system, or transmitted in any form, or by any means, electronic, mechanical, photocopying, or otherwise, without the prior written permission of the publisher, except by a reviewer, who may quote brief passages in a review.

Sophia Institute Press
Box 5284, Manchester, NH 03108
1-800-888-9344
www.SophiaInstitute.com

Sophia Institute Press® is a registered trademark of Sophia Institute.

paperback ISBN 979-8-88911-526-7

ebook ISBN 979-8-88911-527-4

Library of Congress Control Number: 2025934097

First printing

Contents

Part One: The Crime 3

Part Two: Repentance 65

Author's Note (1962 Edition) 151

Endnotes 171

Discussion Questions 173

About the Author 177

I Killed Maria Goretti

PART ONE

The Crime

For the flesh lusteth against the spirit, and the spirit against the flesh. These are at enmity one with another.
—Galatians 5:17

~ 1 ~

ALESSANDRO AWOKE THAT spring morning, as every morning, hating the stench of the Pontine Marshes that burned his nostrils, the stench he had never gotten used to in his two years at Le Ferriere.[1] The dismal odor of decay was to him a symbol of his bondage, of his peasant status, of the unremitting labor and poverty that were his daily lot.

He told himself that smell must be the odor of Hell—if he believed in Hell.

He pulled the rough, wool cover over his head in a futile effort to escape the smell. He thought about staying in bed all day, perhaps pretending he was sick, so he could escape not so much the harsh labors of fields, which his hard young body was used to, but the dreadful reality of his harsh life.

And as he lay there, his thoughts converged on Maria...

"Alessandro," his father's heavy, annoyed voice called, breaking his reverie. "Alessandro, get up at once! Come eat your breakfast! We must get to work early today. There is much to do in the fields."

Unwillingly, but obediently, as always, Alessandro arose from the bed and dressed in his tattered, mud-stained work clothes.

"Good morning, Alessandro," Maria said gaily and musically, as he stepped into the kitchen. "I have made some nice, fresh porridge for you. And there is fresh milk that Mamma got this morning."

She smiled her innocent, lovely, little girl's smile at him, then turned back to her labors at the hearth. He tried to read something into the smile this morning, but he knew it was the same gentle, loving smile she always had for everyone.

Alessandro grunted but said nothing as he sat at the table. He dipped his rough spoon into the porridge but did not eat immediately. He looked at Maria—furtively—as she went busily about her tasks as cook. He looked at her—rather, stared at her—often now, and he saw the beautiful child slowly growing into a woman.

She was not yet twelve, but the hard work of running a house for the two families—her own widowed mother, Assunta, and her brothers and sisters, and for Alessandro and his father—had started to develop and mature her figure. She had long, chestnut blonde hair and a delicacy of features inherited from her comely mother and handsome father. Her delicate beauty was unusual among the peasants of the marshes.

Alessandro noticed all this and the fire inside him grew hotter.

"Alessandro, stop daydreaming!" His father shouted at him, getting up from the table. "We must hurry to the fields. Eat your breakfast and come."

Guiltily, Alessandro began to eat the food, wondering if his father had seen him looking at Maria. But one glance at Giovanni, who was busy picking up his tools, showed Alessandro he had not.

Giovanni went to the stairs, throwing back to his son, "Now, hurry."

Alessandro was alone with Maria now, alone as he hoped to be. Assunta, Maria's mother, was in the barn downstairs doing her morning chores, and the other Goretti children had eaten their breakfast and were out in the fields.

"Marietta," he said tentatively.

"Yes, Alessandro," she answered, not turning from her work.

Crossly, he demanded, "Stop working for a moment, Marietta. I want to talk to you."

She turned to him, still smiling, not abashed at his rough command. "I am sorry, Alessandro. But there is so much to do."

"Marietta..." He faltered.

She looked at him quizzically, still smiling.

"You are getting to be a big girl. I like you," he finally stammered out. But he could say no more. Instead, he took a bag of candies from his pocket and placed it on the table. "These are especially for you," he said.

Maria was obviously touched by this unexpected generosity, he could see. There were a few tears in her eyes, and those tears frightened him.

The girl thanked him profusely. He lowered his gaze and, without speaking another word, left the kitchen.

As he walked down the stone outside stairs, he damned himself as a coward for not speaking, for not demanding from her what he had now begun to consider his right. He had missed his chance, he told himself, and for a moment doubted whether there would ever come a time when he could set free the silent but turbulent spring of passion now held back by the dam of his reticence. But this doubt lasted only a moment. He knew the passion was becoming too strong—and he never made any effort to overcome it—for him to deny it much longer.

The thought of seducing Maria, violently if necessary, was becoming too powerful to permit him to refrain from approaching her. It would be today, he told himself. Today, surely. Today, when he was alone with her again. He would contrive, perhaps, to be apart from the others when she brought his lunch to the fields. Then he would have courage; then he would speak.

But if not today, then tomorrow. Or the day after. But soon.

Alessandro was twenty. He had come to the Pontine Marshes three years before with his father and the Goretti family—Luigi; his wife, Assunta; Maria, the second oldest of the Goretti children; and her brothers and sisters—to sharecrop for Count Mazzoleni.

In his two years at Le Ferriere, Alessandro had come to be considered by the other peasants a good farmer and a mild, calm youth who tended to avoid companionship and mostly kept to his own thoughts. But Alessandro had been discontented and oppressed by the life of the marshes from the first day of his arrival. He had left the sea and its wild and free life—and its fresh, salt smell—to join his father again.

The five years he had spent at sea now seemed a mirage of the past. The sea was to his liking, ever-changing, with a law of its own, beholden to no rules of man. He often remembered the rock-strewn shores, cliffs, reefs, jetties, currents, tides, and restless waves; the bells and whistles, ports, and nets, and the briny smell of kelp and fish. The mariners were not mute plodders chained to the soil and an isolated hut. Their ship was a roving home that took them to Pescara, Vasto, Termoli, and new places where a man could go ashore and walk streets and see life without being censured or questioned. There were no churches at sea, and no commandments to wall one in. The fishermen were a fatalistic lot, given to song and profanity and lust, without shame or recrimination. The life of the sea was pagan. The men enjoyed carnal sin and talked about it with great appetite. The sides of the cabin had pictures of the easy women of the ports.

Alessandro used to listen to the licentious talk of the sailors with an excitement he had never revealed. Captain Gasparre had given him a nickname—the hermit crab.

As for the wants of the stomach, it was not like the peasant's slavish waiting for the earth to rear the wheat. At sea one picked mussels and snails from the rocks, and the nets were always full of lobsters and crabs and myriad edible fish that were simply gutted and flipped over the coals of the brazier or mixed in a pot with oil and herbs for a health-giving meal that asked only for the accompaniment of hard bread and wine.

The sea indicated to Alessandro the dispassionate nature of life: the big fish eating the little flesh for survival, and the big fish in turn vanquished by sharks. He recalled often the dizzy sensation of pulling aboard one of the finny killers of the deep and dealing it death with a club or ax.

On the ship there had been Daniele Pasquale, a boy of the same age as he, who went with the men to the disorderly houses in the ports. Daniele had often tried to get Alessandro to go along, but when it came to making the actual step from desire to reality, Alessandro was always paralyzed. And it was not for religious or moral reasons. The things Alessandro wanted to do he could not bring himself to, as Daniele so easily did. He was aware of the contradiction within him, his sensuous dreams that no one could detect were dear to him, but outwardly he was fastidious about his behavior. Since he had been a child he felt outside of people and families, a creature apart and fated to be alone with his ungovernable impressions and reactions. When he lived with his brother Pietro, he would stay awake at night to listen to Pietro and his wife making love in the next bedroom. Indelicacy both revolted and fascinated him. He asked himself why he could not be like the simple-minded peasants who treated sex as casually as the rutting beasts.

Alessandro had left the sea because of his brother. Pietro had saved his life when, as a mere baby, Alessandro was thrown into the river by his deranged, tormented mother. He owed his life to Pietro, and when the older brother told him to forsake the sea and go to aid their elderly father, who was cropping in the fields, Alessandro obeyed.

Now the life of Le Ferriere had erected invisible walls, jailing him, and at night in his prison, up beyond reach, were the free, blinking islands in the wide seas of the sky. Was there a God up there? What had the Serenelli family done to deserve the string of tragedies—the madness of his mother and his older brother, Gaspare; the hard labor in the fields; empty stomachs much of the time? Was the Serenelli blood cursed?

In the marshes there were no streets and crowds he could anonymously lose himself in, never a carnival or festival where he could safely let his eyes dwell on girls; there was nothing but a few illiterate families whose yoked resignation inspired his contempt, a little church that was just a little church, the fields with which to wrestle, and the overall ponderous silence of the marshes.

Two years before, he had seen Maria's father, Luigi, go from a smiling man with muscles of steel to a raving, wracked malaria patient and then an emaciated and foul corpse within a week. What had sheep-like docility and religion and prayers availed Luigi Goretti? The peasant's life was less secure than that of the oxen. The oxen were carefully fed and stabled. Who was there to feed the sharecroppers? No one but the mute statues of God and the saints — who never answered prayers.

In his limited way, he judged for himself that fate had conspired against him for him to be without mother and family. His excessive sensibility in reprisal demanded that he be an outsider. Since he was little, he had often overheard himself referred to as a "misanthrope." With his acute sense of comparison and questioning, he knew he was different and superior to his fellow peasants. He was painfully conscious that there was a magical law maintaining the comfortable position of the wealthy, and a stark, merciless law keeping the peasant nailed to the earth in poverty. What mysterious law decreed that one man could possess thousands of acres and that hundreds of peasants be subjected to him and his land? Since earliest memory he recalled the unequal contest between his father with landowners: in Paterno, where he was born; then in Paliano, under an eccentric Protestant bishop and landowner, Cappellini; then in Colle Gianturco, where his father teamed up with Luigi Goretti under the vicious landowner, the Sicilian Senator Scelsi; and now under the profligate Count Mazzoleni. The Countess Mazzoleni's cats and lapdogs lived a luxurious life that the peasants would never know. The cost of one of the count's house parties would keep the peasants of Le Ferriere in food for a year. The count bought coffins for the sharecroppers, but there was no doctor in his vast holdings. The count spent fortunes for his recreation but held the widow Assunta to hair-splitting account for every penny he advanced her before the crops were gathered.

What future was there for him, Alessandro? Soon the army would take him against his will. Another trap made by incomprehensible forces. If he did not lose his life in the army, he would be returned to his father and the soil. Was he to wed a peasant, raise more slaves, be in hopeless debt, and end the same as his tragically silent worn-out father or a diseased corpse like Luigi Goretti, leaving behind a crushed widow and defenseless children? He felt lost.

Alessandro was about the only peasant in the area who could read. To read was a secret power, an ability that took him into realms the other peasants were blind to. Though his father spoke harshly to him now and then, he respected Alessandro's wish to read and brought him popular and exciting tabloids and magazines and an occasional best-selling book from Nettuno and Anzio.[2]

The periodicals of the day reflected the government's anticlerical attitudes, fostering criminal and socially inflammatory stories appealing to the masses. It was fashionable to pass down the shocking philosophies of the vain, each of whom vied to outdo the other with the embellishment of horror, all of which was heralded and blazoned in cheap print. The press disseminated this trash with impunity, and, to Alessandro, the fact that words were published established their intrinsic value; made them something persuasive, to be absorbed and, if needs be, imitated. Many of these writers had continental and international reputations, and therefore whatever they said was gospel for Alessandro. He steeped his consciousness in the detailed accounts of crimes of the past and present. He read of a murder witnessed by Stendhal[3] back in the 1830s. A working girl of Civitavecchia[4] was stabbed to death by a mad lover.

"I was struck by the superbly picturesque effect produced by the color of blood on well-gartered stockings on a well-made leg," Stendhal had written. Then at the trial Stendhal proclaimed, "The murderer had more soul in him than all the poets, and more wit than the gentlemen judging him!" And the same Stendhal said of Rome, "At Rome, they know how to hate and wreak vengeance. At Rome, a man knows how to kill and have done with it, and this is why Rome is the finest place in Italy."

Alessandro read the dismal stories seriously. They were crammed with calamities, and horror was piled upon horror. In a crude way he developed his reading ability, and he underlined with a pencil such striking expressions as the following:

"To complete a truly great, frenzied passion, a warm and ardent passion, a crime is a necessity."

"Unless a passion has a fever, a homicidal fury, it is without vigor and beauty."

"The male of the animals maltreat and try to kill the female of the species that resist them."

"Pure passion cannot find counterpoise in religious faith."

"Humanity is animality endowed with the faculty of abstraction and generalization. The sovereign law of the animal is appetite. All species of animals exist only by destruction. The history of humanity is nothing but the continuation and development of this animal fight for life."

"A peasant is a machine who opens the ground to put manure into it, till the day when he lies down in it to become manure himself."

"Crime is not a form of madness, but a wholesome idea, almost a duty, and at the least a noble protest."

"Every man has in his heart a sleeping swine, and the swine often awakens with horrible results. There is no brute so foul and cruel as to rival man in lubricity and cruelty. We are beasts that perish."[5]

The sensationalist literature Alessandro read had been purposely written to stimulate anarchy in the minds of the poor. In the name of physiology, biology, anthropology, and sociology, writers of sensualism treated murder and crime as natural phenomena. Alessandro was incapable of letting it go as blood-tingling entertainment, but morbidly accepted it as a free, desperate, empowering secret code for himself, an answer to his fastidious fears, a silent mental revolt against landowners and the stupidity of toil, poverty, and a religion in which he could not believe.

He was twenty and surfeited with graspless fancies of desire. The photographs of sensuous girls from magazines that he had pasted on the wall beside his bed could never come to life for the wishing. The stories of forbidden fruit no longer nourished him, and self-abuse infuriated him. He would have to transfer imagination to livid, substantial reality. His mind, overly filled with lurid literature, now craved imitation in actual life. All that he had read succeeded in aiding him to become conscienceless and shed the sense of sin from his constant licentious daydreamings and fantasies.

He had read much that ridiculed religion, church, and priests, and he reasoned that if the mockery were not based on truth, it would not have been printed, and therefore the printed word was an oracle. He felt insulated from the mysteries of belief, and he was too completely preoccupied with himself and his physical desire to be moved by faith. He did not know what it meant to try to govern his thoughts. Within the privacy of his mind, he contemplated lusting with the few girls and women of Le Ferriere and nearby Conca, but their self-assured rude ways and vulgar speech offended his concept of himself. The earthiness and loud, dissonant voices of the peasant women upset him. And though he indulged himself with the idea of visiting the paid loose women of Nettuno that the peasant men talked about, he shrank from the thought of doing it.

At first his awareness of Marietta only evoked piety and admiration. She seemed a little nun in rags, a holy, pious little girl, always speaking of God, of Jesus, and the saints. Maria wore castoffs given her by the sympathetic peasant women, a kerchief or shawl around her head and shoulders, and a long-sleeved, nondescript dress. Only her face, work-coarsened hands, and small, bare feet could be seen, and daily her face was smudged by the ashes from the hearth and streaked with sweat from her toil.

It was on the day, shortly before, of Maria's First Communion, when she was dressed in a soft, white dress, that he suddenly saw her with new eyes. That day, a coveting thought came to him about Marietta that made him tremble. He knew it was wrong for that thought to remain, but instead of casting it from his mind, it pleased him to dwell upon it, to see it grow. He began to think of Marietta not as a fatherless child worthy of his protection, but as a growing girl whom he should, by right, possess.

And Maria's very purity challenged him. The very evil of violating that purity fascinated him as if it were a brilliantly colored, dangerous snake. All the rabid and destructive stories he had read helped make of his mind a jungle wherein he safely felt himself the wielder of a potent power against the constraining walls of society and moral order and religion.

The fact that Marietta was not of age, that she was pure, that she was living under the same roof and dependent upon him and his father for the protection and sustenance of herself and her mother and brothers and sisters, that she was — in short — defenseless, only compounded for him the sense of thrill of the wrong that he felt he would inevitably commit. He assured himself of the certainty that he would be the author of the forbidden act, and that it would be safe for him to sin against her even as according to the cruel natural law, which held that the stronger of the beasts asserted its will and needs and desires against the weaker and more innocent.

He knew that with all his great, muscular strength he was timid before reality and feared death. Marietta's invincible belief in God and Heaven confused yet drew him, and he knew he needed her in a way that he could not explain to himself. His powerful hands could express themselves more eloquently than his lips; he felt himself a thinking and physical machine impelled but without direction, as though he were forced to drive wild horses while blindfolded. He could read newspapers and magazines and books, but he could not read himself into belief; faith appeared to him as a nothingness, a labelled blank. But Marietta, who could not tell one printed word from another, could see and read the unseen. The lovely, illiterate, and burgeoning girl had a mysterious inner strength, a fearless core; she had confidence and purpose. He felt he had to prove something to himself, that he must seduce and conquer her strength because, to him, wrong seemed to be the only right. He must break a dread moral law, like a mute who shocks himself into speech.

Stiff-necked pride, not based on social reasons, prevented him from lowering himself to seek a convenient, professional loose woman outside of Le Ferriere, or a woman whose needs were consonant with his own, or a crude, unthinking, indelicate girl of his own age. What appealed to him and attracted him about Maria was the immolation of the pure, which meant to him a secret defiance of society, a perversion of goodness. That to him would be his initiation into sensualism, an act similar to some of the flamboyantly publicized stories of the books he read.

When he accomplished this act, he told himself, he would no longer be the timid, young peasant, but the liberated Alessandro Serenelli, living without concern or regret.

And if Maria resisted him unreasonably long, he would terrorize her into submission. He would threaten her, but there would be no need to carry out the threat. She would give in, for after all, she was only a little, peasant girl. But what if she did resist him, or worse, what if once he had his way with her, she told her mother, and he had to face the recriminations of his family, her family, and the neighbors?

Then, rather than let that happen, he would kill her.

~ 2 ~

MARIA, THOUGH SURPRISED by Alessandro's unexpected gift of candy, attributed it only to friendliness and generosity. She was touched to the point of tears by it. But when Assunta came into the kitchen a short while later, she recalled his words—"I have been thinking about you. You are becoming a big girl. I like you"—and instinctively refrained from telling her mother about it. He said he had been thinking of her. She was only eleven, and he was twenty. Why should he be thinking about her? Gentle Alessandro would not think a wrong thing about her. He was sorry for her, that was all. But he need not be, for she was content and loved the will of God.

Her happy mind soon dismissed the thought as she busied herself with her morning chores.

While working, Marietta would often contemplate the events of her eleven years, and she would especially like to recreate the tender romance of her mother and her dear, dead father—her Babbo. Assunta had told her time and time again how she and Babbo had met, working side by side in the fields of Corinaldo, of his bashfulness and sterling, Catholic nature, his purity of mind, and close adherence to Christian doctrine.

"Sweet child," Assunta would say, "when your Babbo and I were married, we lived in his house in the parish of San Vincento, working the land for Niccola Ciceroni. We moved to the little, stone farmhouse in the Pregiagna section to sharecrop for the landowner Rocci. There, on October 16, 1890, you were given to me by God. The very next day we had you baptized in the Church of San Francesco."

"Yes, Mamma, and I remember the day when I received the Holy Chrism in the Church of Our Mother of Sorrows. And when we went on retreat to the Passionists Fathers in Paliano to hear Mass and sell our eggs and pigeons."

Religious things were always to the forefront of Maria's mind. Early in life she had learned life's purpose from Assunta and Luigi. The reason for being was love, and that with their marriage made in Heaven they were chosen to bring her into the world. Her father and mother were unlettered peasants, but plain and clear were their words telling her of her Creator, of His Son, Jesus, and of His Immaculate Mother, Mary. Marietta's heart was the school that taught her that life was a time of preparation for the everlasting soul's glory in the Kingdom of Christ.

She knew the gift of lips was to speak prayer and gratitude above all else. Monotony and unhappiness did not, could not exist in her home, for there was love. She understood by grace the truth most humans are willfully blind to and flee from, that each morning is the rebirth of God's gift, that each day is to be joyfully lived in the renewal of Christ. Within, she was a column of conscious inner control. She did not question the Christ of her father and mother; in Babbo she saw the good, simple Christ of the fields, and in Assunta she recognized the image of the Queen of the home, Mary. Her secret was gratefulness for the smallest things received, for health, family, the unsung bread and labors, and towering above all, obedience to the Father and the Son and the Holy Ghost. She knew right, she knew it as naturally as she breathed; she saw the right as openly and clearly as she saw the sun. She reached to the concept of God as surely as the infant reaches for the goodness of the breast, as the flowers turn with and upward to the light of the sky.

When but five or six years old, she began to assist Assunta as a tiny mother to her brothers and sisters. "Precious!" Assunta would exclaim to her Luigi, "Precious is our puppy of a Marietta — no one has told her how to help me, but she does it directly as a pigeon homing to its nest!"

The life of her family was a life within a life, the life that the world did not see. The world sees only the exterior life. Her family who lived for God lived an interior life that had depths and sounds and colors of which the external world knew not. The one and only true religion, *the Way*, had been in their blood for nineteen centuries. Their thinking was founded upon the New Covenant. Though they could not read, they understood and took to heart and soul each word of Christ's message as given to them by the priests. More than these words was not necessary. Marietta was always conscious of the aura of Christ in her home, which bestowed the essence of the supernatural upon each moment, each chore, each pleasure, each tear, each smile, each thought. Nothing was burdensome to her, for she lived gratefully in a real and constant state of prayer, thankful for whatever the day brought; and thus she lived through the day. For her family the world was filled with the presence and love of God. Each day began with the simply worded prayer that pointed their lives toward Him. Every night, the family Rosary bound them with golden chains about His feet. Their poverty was not too hard to bear when they remembered how the Son of God was born in a stable. Their suffering from heat or cold or hunger was softened by the memory of a tortured God-man hanging on a Cross. Living their humble lives for Him and in His name was a magnificent adventure, a tremendous love story. And on Sundays and Holy Days, she and her family, dressed in their Sabbath best, could see the Son of God lifted up again on the altar of their little church of the Annunziata in Conca, reminding them of His love and His abiding Presence.

Thus, life was perfectly understandable to Marietta. She never compared her Babbo with those who had greater comforts and means, and did not think of him as a failure. Babbo had given his family all his love and his life. And in her mind, God did not consider him a failure any more than He thought that the carpenter, Joseph of Galilee, was a failure who could find no better birthplace than a stable for God's Son.

Babbo had loved and served God with all his strength. He had taken the children sent to him and taught them that the only real success in life is to be a success with God. God the Creator was the only One whose favor was to be sought, for sooner or later men were as withered leaves, ashes, and the wind. Babbo had kept away from sin. He had performed faithfully the duties of his state of life. To God and to her, her Babbo was a great man.

She learned early that to live for God was deep and stirring, with always a sense of endless adventure. And it was not a dream world. It enabled her to see everything in its true context. That they moved penniless like hungry gypsies from Corinaldo to Colle Gianturco and then to the bleak isolation of Le Ferriere did not perturb her. Places and walls and floors and roofs did not make a home, but only love, and love was free as it was poured down by Him from above; it had only to be wanted, cherished, and reached for. She never owned a rag doll to play with. But she did not need one. She had her baby brothers and sisters to care for, and her Mamma and Babbo, and she loved them all to distraction. Her child's heart was brimful of love for everyone, for she had been told that God was love. And she said to herself, "I will love for I am she who can love." Early she was capable of the ecstasy of self-forgetfulness, and she would say in her little girl's prayers, "I love, I obey, I smile, Dearest Lord; I ask for no more."

Each evening, she was the first to run to Babbo as he came home from the fields, and when he swung her astride his shoulders, she laughed and shouted until she was breathless with happiness. When he died of malaria, she was sick with sorrow, but her grief was neither selfish nor fruitless. She was nine years old, but realistic above literates and sages; she realized all life was not contained in and limited by living flesh. She saw her handsome Babbo turn into a foul corpse, but she knew all the living would have to die sooner or later; a brief or long life was an infinitesimal measure of eternity; this world was not and never could be the goal of the heart, the lasting abode of love, the final home of the soul. To her young, deep mind, it was not right or logical that love ended with the destruction of her Babbo. He had simply been called by the Lord to Paradise, ahead of the others in the family, and would be watching and waiting for them. Babbo was with the Son of God, Jesus; otherwise being had no sense. His death brought her completely close to God and rooted her soul strongly in Paradise where Babbo was. Nothing could hurt her then.

What could hurt her, though, was the thought of anyone doing something that would keep them from Paradise. In the stores of Conca, at the fountain, and at chance village gatherings, peasant boys and girls, and even grown-ups, freely used profane and immoral speech that shocked and saddened her.

Assunta knew, and advised her, "My puppy, whenever you hear bad words, let it go in one ear and out the other."

"Mamma," she replied, "I would rather bite my tongue than speak an unclean word."

While working in the home so many hours of the day, Marietta looked forward to the Sunday mornings when she could receive Holy Communion. In that moment, she was nourished and rewarded by Christ, the family of saints, and her beloved Babbo. She dreaded to think of ever losing through sin, particularly the sin of impurity, that grace and her intimate relationship with Paradise. Mass and Communion in nearby Conca at the Church of the Annunziata was available for eight months during the year. Religious services began there with the feast of All Saints on November 1 and terminated the following June 29 with the feast of Sts. Peter and Paul. Most of the population was comprised of the migrant peasants, who feared the malarial season and, following the feast of Sts. Peter and Paul, fled home to the safe air of the hills and mountains. From July to November, Marietta, accompanied either by Assunta or her godmother and neighbor Teresa Cimarelli, walked the blazing, dusty seven miles to receive the precious Holy Communion at Our Lady of Graces Church in Nettuno.

Holy Communion was the Sabbath feast that sustained her for the coming week.

~ 3 ~

ALESSANDRO'S CHANCE TO approach Maria came that night, after dinner.

Giovanni Serenelli gruffly ordered Angelo, Maria's brother, and Marietta to feed the oxen in the stalls below their living quarters. Angelo complained that he was tired from his day in the fields, and Giovanni raised his hand in anger at Angelo. But Alessandro intervened saying, "I will help Marietta tend the beasts."

As they went down the stairs together, his heart beat wildly at the thought that tonight would be the time. Tonight he would become the living Alessandro Serenelli, freed from the conventions that his life as a peasant had built around him.

When they were alone in the barn, he whispered, "Marietta, we are alone. We can do anything. No one will catch us here. No one will know what we are doing."

In her innocence, she did not understand, and asked, "What do you mean, Alessandro? What is there to do that no one should know?"

He blurted out what he wanted of her. His ugly words seared her mind. She understood immediately why in the past months he had been so solicitous of her, had defended her against his father's complaints and beatings, had helped her with chores and given her candy.

Her face was filled with horror.

He persisted—lamely, "I am not a stranger to you. You have known me for three years. I am not trying to force you—or take advantage of you. But you do belong to me. Do as I say and there is nothing for you to fear."

She cringed from him as he reached his arm out to grab hers. "No, Alessandro, you cannot do this. It is not right, it is sinful. Think of your soul, Alessandro."

"I will not give up," Alessandro said, angry now. But he was still too timid to make a move toward her.

"Babbo," she prayed aloud, "Babbo, watching me from Heaven, save Alessandro from sin."

Alessandro was bewildered now. His goal was in sight, he had made his move, he had proposed his deed to Marietta. Should he force his will on her now, here in the barn?

But Assunta's voice was calling from the outside stairway: "Marietta! Puppy, finish down there and help me with the kitchen work, as I can hardly stand from fatigue!"

Marietta turned and ran breathlessly up the stairs, fighting back the tears.

"What is the matter, child?" Assunta asked when she arrived in the kitchen. "Your face is white as death. Are you sick?"

"I'm all right, Mamma," the child said.

How could she tell Assunta what Alessandro had proposed? Babbo in Heaven knew it, knew what Alessandro had said in the barn. But how could she tell her poor mother? Did not Assunta have enough to worry about? Good Alessandro would surely steer himself clear of the dangerous and evil idea. She would pretend he had never said those terrible words to her. But coming from Alessandro, whom she had so implicitly trusted and cherished as a big brother, those words could not easily be forgotten. Was there a possibility Alessandro might force her to his desire? She who had never been afraid of injury or death now shuddered. Her soul, the soul she had kept so pure for the life eternal, was all that mattered to her.

As soon as she could, she finished the work in the kitchen, went to her bedroom, and knelt in prayer—for Alessandro's soul and for God's protection of her own purity.

That night, Alessandro had approached the definition of life. He had acted. He had broken his shell and spoken aloud his want of Marietta. Now he could not and would not retreat from his purpose. He would, he must, follow through and succeed in seducing her. He had made the first steps toward that exciting bestial reality, and the effect heightened his sense of thrill. He was shaking and challenging the dormant Alessandro to smash the smothering pattern of his dull and monotonous peasant existence.

There would be another time; and then, he would not fail.

On Sunday, a few days later, he managed to approach her again. She had been religiously avoiding him since that night in the barn. But while harvesting the bean crop, he managed to work close to her, and when he saw that Assunta, his father, and the others were beyond hearing, he said, "I am determined more than ever than you shall let me have my way. You carry on as if I were the devil. Do not be afraid of me, for there is no harm in what I want. Are you not grateful and flattered that I like you and want you? Why do you not answer me?"

Marietta worked on, avoiding his glance, not speaking, ready to run if he touched her.

"Why do you not answer?" he asked again, half demanding, half pleading, for her silence frightened him.

"Alessandro, please, I am just a child."

"Without my father and me, your family will starve. Nobody will see after a widow and six children. You are obligated to me. You are mine for whatever I desire. Marietta, be reasonable, do not resist me for long and provoke my hatred, for I vow it will go bad for you."

He reached out to grab her, but she shrank away.

Angrily, he declared, "I will have my way, Marietta. Some day. And I promise you, if you become silly enough to tell on me, if you tell Assunta or anyone else, I'll have my father throw you all out of the house."

Another time, during the harvesting of the corn, Giovanni ordered her to stay behind Alessandro and gather the ears into baskets. Alessandro looked about him, and, seeing the others at a distance, he pulled Marietta in among the tall grain. As he held her, she dreaded the disgrace of outcry, thinking of her family—their shelter and food, and equally, of the future of Alessandro's soul.

"Alessandro," she pleaded, "for the love of God, do not mar our souls—please let me go!"

He shook her and demanded, "Why are you so stubborn, Marietta?"

With tearful eyes, she replied, "Do not misunderstand, Alessandro. You have been a good brother to me and a dear son to Mamma, for which Jesus will bless you. But please,

Alessandro, do not visit the stain of sin upon us. Alessandro, have mercy."

He tried to kiss her, but she struggled free. Panting, she covered her face with her hands and wept, "For shame — shame, Alessandro."

Defeated, he picked up his brush hook from the ground and viciously lopped at the corn. "Damn you, Marietta, I will give you one more chance! If you frustrate me again, by God, I will hack you down like corn."

In the field the following day, Alessandro saw two carabinieri[6] from the Cisterna riding toward him on horseback. His knees weakened; Marietta had told, he thought, and now the police are coming to arrest me.

He would deny he had tried to seduce her and that he had threatened to kill her. Marietta would not be able to prove her charge. After all, she was just eleven, and what was the word of a child against his? But still, the sight of the stern faces and the Napoleonic hats and dark blue uniforms made him quake. If he had a rifle, he would rather shoot them dead than face them. In that moment, he had an immense hatred for all law and all uniforms.

The mustachioed, iron-faced, older carabiniere dismounted by him. Orlando Ruggeri, the younger officer, noting Alessandro's consternation, smiled: "Youth, be not disturbed. We are merely checking for the military service. What is your name, and of what class are you?"

"Alessandro Serenelli," answered Alessandro with relief, "of the class of '82."

"You live in the ancient farmhouse of Le Ferriere with your father, the old fellow, and the family of the deceased Goretti? Your sire and the Goretti widow sharecrop together this holding of the Count Mazzoleni?"

Alessandro remembered to remove his hat, and then answered anxiously, "That is right, sir carabiniere."

Carabiniere Pierattini wrote down the facts and said, "Your class is of age for his majesty's service. You would do well to present yourself to the military post of Nettuno tomorrow for examination."

"Yes, sir carabiniere," replied Alessandro respectfully.

Carabiniere Ruggeri asked him how he felt about being a soldier and added that it was not a bad life.

Alessandro lowered his eyes. "Sir Carabiniere, I cannot truthfully say whether it pleases me or displeases me. All my life I have done what I have been told to do. I suppose I am accustomed to that, and therefore, I do what I must."

Carabiniere Ruggeri gave Alessandro a friendly clap on the back. "If you are taken, accept it in good spirit. You are a rugged one—the army will be a lark for you, and then you will return to your farming. It is the way things go. Young Serenelli, good luck to you."

Alessandro mused that perchance he might be sent into the navy and live on the unrooted ships sailing the mysterious seas and enjoy the wild freedom of the sailor during stays in ports. He half-hoped it would come about and release him from his compelling decision to seduce Marietta.

His rationalizing mood did not last. At the military post in Nettuno, he was examined, passed, and unceremoniously told he would be called into the army. In the army, he would be one of thousands of voiceless, regimented men, ordered about, made to do detestable labors; he would be more confined and exploited than ever, and there was also the possibility of being injured or killed in one of the king's African military ventures. Now he would be in daily suspense wondering when he would be taken into that trap. He berated himself for living only in imagination and not having the courage to rebel and explode like the daring characters in stories.

He was the hermit snail who dreamed of being a predatory lion.

~ 4 ~

WITH THE FIRST days of July, the fava bean crop, which Count Mazzoleni sold to the military post at Nettuno, had ripened, dried hard in the sun, and was harvested.

By now, Alessandro's mania to seduce Marietta, abetted by his conception of life as being nothing but bestial, was rapidly overpowering him. The labors of the field were now an abomination to him, taunting him.

The 1st and 2nd of July were hot and showed evidence that the following days would be hotter. The nights of the 3rd and 4th were sleepless for Alessandro. The stars were silent, the marshes silent, the darkness silent. A few yards away, in her bedroom, was Marietta, whom he had to have at any cost now. Was she asleep? Were his threats and temptations having the effect on her that he wished for? Or was she, in her disdain for him, seeking futile refuge in prayer? There was no such place as Heaven, he told himself, and if there were, it would be useless against his compulsion.

With the dawn of July 5, Alessandro arose from his bed of torment, choking with desire. He said, half-aloud, "Today there must be an end! Marietta consents, or I shall kill her!"

That morning, Marietta had been, as usual, the first to arise. She made the fire in the hearth, cooked the pot of wheat cereal, dressed the children, and led them in morning prayer. Giovanni Serenelli came into the kitchen, his gaunt face yellow for he was sick with malaria. At the breakfast table, Alessandro's stare followed Marietta unguardedly now, but somehow Assunta did not notice anything foreboding about his appearance.

"Assunta," said Giovanni in a sickly voice, "this will be an inferno of a day. The Cimarellis are going to thrash beans. We too will work in the barn and do likewise."

Teresa Cimarelli, who lived in the adjoining farmhouse, entered the kitchen with a gift for Marietta—a faded red, but still wearable, blouse and skirt sent to Marietta by the Casoni woman whose daughter had outgrown the garments. Teresa insisted Marietta change from her dun-colored, long, heavy dress. When Marietta returned from her room wearing the blouse and skirt, Teresa and Assunta were delighted. Teresa removed her kerchief and placed it over Marietta's chestnut-blonde tresses.

"Tomorrow is the feast of the Most Precious Blood," Marietta said. "Godmother Teresa, do walk with me to Our Lady of Graces in Nettuno. I can hardly wait for the hour of Communion."

"Yes, dear Marietta," Teresa responded, "though the sun will scorch us, I will be happy to accompany you. For I am sure Jesus loves you as much as you love Him."

The Serenellis and the Gorettis descended to the huge barn below, where high mounds of fava beans awaited the threshing. Marietta placed her sister, Ersilia, who was four, and baby Teresa in a safe corner where she could watch them while she worked. Alessandro and his father hitched the two pair of oxen to the carts. The threshing was primitive. The oxen were reined about in a continuous circle; the bean pods were scattered on the barn floor, and the unshod hooves of the animals and the iron cart wheels shredded them. The pods and beans were then scooped up from the clean floor with wooden shovels and dumped into large baskets. Bean threshing, not being strenuous, was done with a customary spirit of gaiety, with all taking turns driving the oxen with a harmless whip and shrill shouts.

But Alessandro was not gay. The rehearsals and variations of lust's violence in Alessandro's mind had been too long fiction; today, they must become reality. The imagined had to be concretely realized. The teasing dreams, the carnal visions had to burst from the cave of his mind and harden into reality in his hands and before his eyes. "Today," he said to himself, "today." He read lust into the sweltering day, and all things about him spoke to him of lust—the breathless, sun-broiled air, the humidity, the nutty smell of crushed fava beans, the scent of human sweat. Lust, said the smells; lust, said earth and marsh gas; lust, said the pulsing wet heat. Lust!

At noon, Marietta carried little Teresa and led Ersilia from the barn and up the outside stairway to the kitchen to prepare lunch. She boiled a pot of homemade spaghetti in the hearth and simmered a sauce of garlic in olive oil, then made a salad of chicory greens mixed with oil, salt, and vinegar. Soon the others came up and gathered at the large, crude table, bowed their heads in grace, and listlessly partook of the frugal lunch.

After lunch, the sun was at its highest, and it was the hour for siesta. Assunta, fatigued, her clothes drenched with perspiration, went to the bedroom for her needed rest. Giovanni

Serenelli, shaking with a recurring malarial seizure, went down to the shaded arcade under the stairway and flung himself upon some sacks of beans to sleep. From his room, Alessandro could hear Marietta making peace between Angelo and Mariano, her brothers, who had gotten into a quarrel, the sounds of her kitchen chores, and her teaching of the catechism to Ersilia.

In the last few weeks, Maria had religiously avoided being alone with him. Her instinct had sensed his maneuvers in that direction. Now he devised a plan that would possibly keep her away from the others for a while. He would use the pretext of a torn shirt to be patched.

As Assunta and her boys were about to leave the kitchen and return to the threshing, Alessandro said to Marietta with disguised calm, "Oh, Marietta, my only other shirt is torn and must be repaired now."

Marietta did not raise her eyes to him or acknowledge his request. Assunta innocently admonished her for what she thought was lack of respect and appreciation for Alessandro, and she concluded, "Marietta, you surprise me. Listen and do quickly what good Alessandro tells you."

Marietta limited her response to the terse question, "Where is the shirt?"

Alessandro answered, "Look in my room. You will find it on the bed, and there is also a piece to patch it with."

Without looking at him, Marietta said, "Very well."

As the others were about to go down to the barn again, Marietta wanted Ersilia to stay with her. Alessandro held his breath until Ersilia said, "There is no fun up here, and I want to be in the barn and ride the cart and shout at the oxen with the others."

Marietta was left alone with baby Teresa, asleep on a pallet in the kitchen.

~ 5 ~

IT WAS THREE o'clock. Alessandro knew that this was the time. The occasion was opportune. His father was ill and prostrate in the arcade under the stairway, everyone else was happily threshing in the barn. The shouts of Assunta's children, the stamping of the oxen hoofs, the piercing creaking of the cart wheels, the popping and cracking of the dried bean pods would blanket any sounds from above where Marietta was.

He halted his cart, jumped down, and said to Assunta: "I am drowning in sweat. Take over the driving of my cart. I have something to do. Yes, I am going above for a brief while — to fetch a handkerchief."

Assunta, clean of heart and spirit, did not connect his going above with any evil intent. She nodded, had Mariano strew the beans in the path of the oxen in her stead, and climbed up into the seat of Alessandro's cart.

As he hastened around the corner of the barn, Alessandro saw Marietta on the landing of the stairway. She was seated on a low stool, intently sewing the patch on his shirt. By her side and asleep on a blanket was Teresa. Marietta, with her lovely face and tresses, her shapely form and limbs, was a beautiful, small woman. The instant sight of her sealed his resolve. He automatically checked to see in what state of awareness his father was, looked in under the stairway, and asked, "How do you feel?" Giovanni made no answer. Alessandro turned back to the foot of the stairway. As he began to walk up the sixteen brick stairs, Marietta glanced down at him momentarily, then went back to her sewing. When he got to the platform landing, she modestly moved her bare feet so that he could get by to the kitchen door without brushing against her.

Marietta heard the clinking of metal from within as he sought the brush hook from the tool chest in the tiny corridor beneath his and his father's room. Her heart quickened with premonition. He had climbed the stairs like someone stalking in a dream. She was about to pick up sleeping Teresa and hurry down to her family when Alessandro opened the inward-swinging kitchen door.

The broad blade of the brush hook was jammed between his belt and waist. The massive muscles of his arms were quivering, his giant chest heaving uneasily, and sweat was pouring from his head down over his face.

To Marietta, this was not the true and real Alessandro, this was the sin-poisoned, soul-imperiled Alessandro whose eyes said "sin or die." If only someone would suddenly come from the barn, she thought frantically.

"Maria, come here," Alessandro commanded.

With drying voice she asked, "What for?"

"Come inside to me!" he whispered fiercely.

She shook her head. The shaking of her head was the no-saying wall of society and moral order that had kept him in his imagined prison, the denying barrier that had to give way, that he would have to smash at and destroy.

Then Marietta made a move to rush down the stairway. But he lunged at her, grabbed her arms with his iron-hard hands, pulled her into the kitchen, and kicked the door closed behind him. He held her face close to his and spat out the ugly words of his want.

He felt she had no recourse but to submit to him, so his fingers relaxed. She backed away from him, praying, hoping, that miraculously he would let her go without disgrace or harm. She was thinking of her father, of Jesus, of Assunta. Alessandro followed her about relentlessly. He had gone this far; now he had to go all the way. And he had to hurry, before he was intercepted. Fear would make her give in. It could not occur to him she was then no longer thinking of her safety but of preserving his soul for Paradise.

As she moved backward about the kitchen with him getting ever closer to her, she whispered vigorously, "No, Alessandro. What are you doing, Alessandro? Alessandro, you do not know what you are doing. It is not you who are doing this. You will go to Hell. It is a sin. God does not wish this!"

He backed her up against the closed kitchen door and pinned her against it with his arms pushed to the door on both sides of her. He caught her in his arms and tried to throw her to the floor. But she struggled with him wildly, a strength coming to her almost equal to his own.

And he knew then that if she did not willingly submit, he could not have her. He took his arms from her, pulled the brush hook from his belt, and pressed its curved point against her breast.

Pantingly, hoarsely, he declared, "This split moment—submit or die!"

Instead of Alessandro's twistened, maddened face before her, she saw the white, flaming command: "Death, but not sin!"[7]

"No, Alessandro, never!" And she cried out, "Mamma! Help! Mamma!"

This ultimate repulse and then the alarm of her voice brought on his insensate fury. He wielded the brush hook and struck her madly, hacking her breast and stomach and back blindingly again and again as though he could slaughter her over and over. The murderous blade struck her fourteen times.

"Mamma, God — God, I'm dying!" she screamed.

It all took place within seconds. Bleeding, disheveled, mortally wounded, Marietta collapsed on the floor.

Alessandro raised his weapon for the destroying blow.

She moaned, and angelically, sadly, said, "I forgive you ... for you do not know what you are doing. Your soul, your soul ... Alessandro, I forgive you. I want your soul with me in Paradise."

Her eyes closed and she became motionless. Alessandro let the brush hook fall harmlessly to his side.

Marietta's cries had awakened baby Teresa, whose frightened screams stirred Alessandro to reality. He thought Marietta was dead. Now all the dreams and desire that had driven him to this act fled from him, leaving him weak and spent. He had sought a change in his life. Now the change had come. Alessandro Serenelli would never be the same.

He heard his father from below fretfully calling to Marietta to look after and quiet the baby. He knew he would soon be found out. Maybe he could go down to the threshing as though nothing had happened. There were no witnesses. But the baby would not stop crying until someone came to her.

Then, surely Marietta's body would be discovered. He was not a liar—he was too proud to lie. Attempted escape would be futile. There were no trees nor houses in the marshes in which to hide. Besides, he was without will now and did not want to do anything. The natural, the inevitable consequences would have to follow. What had happened, happened. And what was going to happen would happen. He walked toward his room, paused to throw the brush hook behind the tool chest, and, turning to Marietta's inert form, sighed bitterly, "Why did you not submit to me!"

~ 6 ~

Marietta's healthy, young being strove bravely not to perish. A semiconsciousness returned to her. She struggled painfully and managed to crawl to the door, reach up, turn the knob, and open it. She cried out, her pleas for aid interspersed with the howling of the infant, who had toddled to her feet and was in danger of falling down the stairway.

"Giovanni," Marietta called out with anguish, "Come up! Your Alessandro has hurt me…"

There was a lull in the noisy threshing down in the barn, and Teresa's cries reached Assunta. Was Marietta neglecting Teresa? It was not like her to do that. Assunta went to the small barn window on the stairway side of the building and called up with all her might, "Marietta, why does Teresa howl? What has gone wrong? Why do you not answer your mother, Marietta! You are trying my patience."

Disturbed by Marietta's silence, Assunta fitfully ordered Mariano to go soothe and care for Teresa. Giovanni blasphemed at the annoying ruckus above and totteringly climbed the stairway to put a stop to it. Mariano by then was just a step behind. As they reached the landing, Mariano picked up Teresa, who stopped crying.

The kitchen door was partly open. Giovanni looked in and said, "Marietta, why did you call me? Are you here?" He could not see her. She had lost consciousness, and her limp form was lodged behind the door. He had to push the door hard to get in.

The sight of Marietta lying in pools of blood stupefied Giovanni and brought from him an exclamation of horror. Mariano, curious, came in; then turned suddenly and, still holding Teresa, fled down the stairs in terror. When he got down to the farmyard, he placed Teresa down on the ground and ran hysterically toward the road, not knowing where he was going.

Giovanni shrank back helplessly from the form of Marietta, rushed out to the landing, and, cupping his hands to his mouth, called for the Cimarellis to leave their barn and come up.

Below, Assunta, sensing fright in the tone of Giovanni's voice, rushed out of the barn. Angelo, Mariano, Sandrino, and Ersilia had been with her. Had something happened to Marietta? Or baby Teresa?

Mario Cimarelli and his brother came from their nearby barn. "What is it?" Mario called up.

"Come up quickly!" shouted Giovanni, "And Assunta, especially you! My God! My God!"

"Madonna," cried Assunta, as she trailed the Cimarellis up the stairway, "what has happened in my house?"

Mario picked Marietta up before Assunta could clearly see her and hurriedly carried her to her bed. Assunta right behind then saw Marietta deathlike, her rose blouse and skirt torn and streaming deep red from many wounds. Had a wild beast found her alone to do this? Had a madman come invisibly and wrought this ghastly deed, then vanished into the air? She knelt in prayer and cried, "O God, save my child!"

Mario ordered his wife, Teresa, to fetch vinegar, salt, and clean rags, and do all she could for Marietta. Then he dashed out and ran to Conca to Count Mazzoleni for help. As Teresa opened Marietta's blouse, the awful wounds were revealed. Assunta bit her fingers and cried, "Teresa, my daughter has been killed!" Assunta's mind blackened and she sank to the floor.

Teresa Cimarelli's tears mingled with Marietta's blood as she tried vainly to staunch its flowing with rags soaked in salted wine vinegar. "O Mother of Christ," she cried, "is there room for another wound in this beautiful child?"

Teresa's sister-in-law applied vinegar to Assunta's nostrils and revived her.

The Cimarelli's children, meanwhile, had begun to spread the alarming news to the few families beyond the bridge and fountain in Le Ferriere, and the men and women and children of the Casoni, Albertini, and Comparini families came running over the sun-drenched road to the Goretti farmhouse. With much commotion and consternation, they sought to see Marietta and to learn what happened.

Giovanni Serenelli sat dumbly in the kitchen. Hugh Rita Comparini said suspiciously, "Old Giovanni, you say you were resting beneath the stairway. How could the assassin go up and down the stairs without your knowing?"

"I am ill with the cursed malaria," Giovanni replied, "and was asleep until I heard Marietta call my name." But Giovanni was trembling. He knew it was Alessandro who had gone up the stairway. Alessandro had first paused to inquire how he felt, and Giovanni had not bothered to answer his son. At any time now someone would notice Alessandro's absence from the woeful scene, and if Marietta regained consciousness, the crushing truth about his son would come to light.

Teresa Cimarelli did not know which of the atrocious wounds to tend to first. There were no proper antiseptics at hand other than the peasants' usual vinegar and salt, which aroused wounds to burning pain. The pain shocked Marietta to consciousness. Seeing Marietta's eyes opening, Assunta said, "God's love, do not die. How terribly do you feel? What happened? Who has done this to you?"

Retching gripped Marietta, and she could not answer at once. But in a moment, she managed to whisper, "I cannot breathe. Loosen my clothes, undress me . . ." And then, in pity of her poor mother, "Mamma, you must not bear the sight of my wounds."

"I cannot leave you, my puppy," Assunta cried.

Turning to Teresa, Marietta whispered, "I want to be alone with you and Mamma. Have everybody leave us."

When they were alone, she said supplicatingly, "For the love of God, do not let Alessandro near me. O Alessandro, how sad you have made your life! You have sought Hell, but you must yet strive for Heaven."

Teresa and Assunta asked, "Then was it Alessandro who did this to you?"

Marietta nodded. "Yes, it was Alessandro. He wanted to force me to commit an ugly sin with him. I said 'No, no, no.'"

The truth, almost unbelievable, stunned the two women. They could not speak. But when Teresa removed Marietta's skirt and her deep stomach gashes were bared, Assunta put her hands to her head and screamed, "Alessandro! Alessandro Serenelli is the assassin who butchered my little girl!"

Alessandro's room was oven hot. The pictures on the walls of glamorous women and of spectacular criminals were now ironic. He had done something of enormity, a grave act. His life had left the realm of fiction and was now closing in on him with stark reality. He had shattered the dam of convention and was no more the unnoticed snail of a peasant. He would soon be swept up by a vast torrent. He was now Alessandro Serenelli, the outlaw, one of history's catalogue of criminals. Struggling against the swirling fate he had created would be utterly useless. He had bolted the door, but he could not lock out that fate, nor halt the unfolding drama beyond the door.

Now desire, which had intrigued him and lured him, had gone, leaving him a culprit. The flesh that had been his lord and master was now a burden and a hazard that he could not hide. His last and impenetrable refuge would have to be mute, sullen, bitter rage against his idealistic little victim and the punishment that lay before him. The hand of man's law would soon garner him, and there was a mordant relief in the thought. Now society would designate his destiny. He would be the responsibility of the criminal court. But with the battering down of the bolted door, he would emerge a publicized personality of fate.

From the temporary security of his room, he had listened to his father's discovery of Marietta and the ensuing turmoil of horrified voices. He could distinguish those who were wildly calling for help, the grieving, lame tone of his father, who surely realized that he was the guilty one, the fearful and plaintive voices of Assunta and Teresa. He knew the make-up of his fellow peasants. Within a short time they would excitedly relay on foot the fact of the bloody happening to the sparse villages of Conca, Compomorto, Carano, Cisterna, and then to the cities of Nettuno and Anzio, and those hearing would leave their work and flock to the scene of the crime.

When Assunta screamed his name as the butcher of Marietta, he shivered. Then he heard his name re-echoed by those gathering in the farmyard. He heard his father pathetically protest to Assunta, "Your son Sandrino is also called Alessandro. He and not my Alessandro did it!" And he heard Assunta cry, "What? My seven-year-old Sandrino who adores his sister? He was by my side in the cart."

Then Giovanni knocked repeatedly on the door, and in a broken voice said, "Alessandro, open. Alessandro are you there? Alessandro, are you ill? Has something come over you? Please come out and tell the truth—that you are innocent..."

But Alessandro claimed the right to remain silent. With his single act of violence, he had removed himself forever from the simple, unlettered dominion of his poor father.

Peasants were gathering in the farmyard and clamoring to get their hands on him. The docile peasants really would not do anything to him on their own. They would shout and curse him, but they would wait for the law to take over. He thought, "It would be better for me if Marietta lived." But he could not hope for that. Nor could he really care for his own safety, for care had left him, and all he felt was aloneness and stolid bitterness, even against himself.

On the Conca road sounded galloping horsemen and fast moving vehicles. And into the farmyard came Count

Mazzoleni's carriage, the count's mounted private armed guard, and the Red Cross ambulance from Carano.

Alessandro heard the newcomers in the kitchen a few feet from his door. Count Mazzoleni called to him to come out peacefully. Though he knew that any second he would have to face people and the world, he did not answer.

The huge peasant woman Rita Comparini exclaimed with an oath, "Why wait for him? I will fetch the beast myself!" She hurled herself against the door and broke it open. Alessandro was on his bed. The Comparini woman lunged toward him, but Giovanni intervened. With perfect ease and as though nothing had happened, Giovanni placed his hand on his son's forehead and asked him, "What have you? A fever?"

Simulating a voice of illness, Alessandro said, "Yes, Father."

Rita Comparini shouted, "Turn him over to the outraged Christians in the farmyard below, and we will give him the fever he deserves!"

Mazzoleni's guards stood sentinel with drawn pistols at the entrance to Alessandro's room until the arrival of Carabinieri Ruggeri and Pierattini from Cisterna. The carabinieri immediately pulled Alessandro to his feet and clapped the ponderous yoke-like iron handcuffs about his wrists.

Alessandro thought of the time when he was a lad in Torrette and had seen a prisoner on the streets handcuffed, the sight of the iron about the man's wrists leaving a brutal and revolting impression upon him throughout the years. His own hands now were iron-bound, and he was being introduced into the ritual of his new career as an apprehended criminal.

As Drs. Baliva and Bartoli administered first aid to Marietta, she hovered in and out of consciousness, whispering prayers to Jesus, the Madonna, her beloved Babbo. The doctors reported to the carabinieri that their examination revealed four minor and fourteen major wounds, four of which were of a fatal nature. They said she could not possibly survive, and that they wondered what miracle was keeping her alive.

The carabinieri asked Alessandro where he had hidden his weapon. He refused to speak. Count Mazzoleni then loudly and severely demanded Alessandro tell him what he had done with the weapon. And without emotion, Alessandro said in a low voice, "It is behind the tool chest that stands outside of my door in the little corridor."

The carabinieri then led Alessandro to the pools of Marietta's blood on the kitchen floor and confronted him with the blood-stained brush hook. To their questions he answered, "I confess to nothing. I stand mute."

They were words he had read in a story.

Two more carabinieri arrived from Nettuno. Assunta was brought to face Alessandro for the formal procedure of identification. The viewers fully expected she would denounce him, but Assunta pressed her hands to her breast and said, "Alessandro, Marietta was an obedient, respectful little sister to you. Her hands cooked and served your food. You drank the water she carried from the fountains. Her willing hands washed your linen. Her prayers were for all under this roof. Alessandro, I had a mother's heart toward you, and you were as one of my own sons. What demon possessed you to butcher my child?"

Alessandro bowed his head and remained silent.

And as the carabinieri began to take Alessandro away, Assunta cried out, "Why did you do it? Did this have to be?"

The ragged peasants—men, women, and children—beheld the ragged, barefooted prisoner descend the stairway. There were those there who knew him, and there were strangers. Many of them carried tools of their labors, a hoe, a sickle, a shovel, which they brandished as weapons of retribution. They surrounded the four carabinieri, roaring curses against Alessandro. The policemen sternly warned the peasants to keep their distance. The carabinieri tied one of the lengthy reins to Alessandro's handcuffs and the other to a saddle, and, while Carabiniere Ruggeri remained at the farmhouse, the three others on horseback and Alessandro on foot, being rapidly pulled behind, set off for Nettuno.

Inside the farmhouse, the doctors did their utmost to keep Marietta alive. Finally, they decided to risk moving her to the small hospital in Nettuno.

The peasants watched with piety and profound sympathy as the beautiful child was borne on a litter to the ambulance.

~ 7 ~

ALL OF NETTUNO knew what happened in Le Ferriere to a little girl named Maria Goretti, and most of the inhabitants of the town waited in the streets for the ambulance to appear, that they might wave blessings and prayers to the little martyr of purity.

Flaming dust was falling, and from the Mediterranean came the hot, stifling breath of the southeast wind, the sultry African sirocco. Passionist fathers and people in the street watched the Red Cross wagon of mercy pulled by two white horses as it raced past Our Lady of Graces and up along the sea wall toward the military post, the railroad station, and the jail, and swerved in to the Hospital Orsenigo of the Welfare Brothers.

Surgeons Perotti and Onesti were ready for Marietta in the operating room as soon as she arrived. Dr. Bartoli quickly informed them of Marietta's grave and surely hopeless condition. The doctors then suggested to the hospital chaplain, Fr. Martino Guijarro, that Marietta's confession be heard before the operation. Padre Guijarro went to Assunta in the adjoining room. Assuming the least alarming aspect possible, he asked, "Woman, we are Christians, is it not so?"

"Father, and what else ..."

"Then, shall I hear your child's confession before the operation?"

"The Madonna has let her arrive here alive ... Yes, first of all, hear her confession."

Within a few moments, the priest heard Marietta's sweet, innocent confession. At the end, she gasped, "Good father, forgive me for the deep hurt this day has brought to my mother. Forgive me. Mamma did not need, she did not deserve this."

Marietta's life was a fragile, dissolving skein, and the burden of anesthesia upon it was out of the question. Under the arc light, the surgeons labored heroically to stave off encroaching death. Marietta's ripped heart, her punctured lungs were unreachable to their skill; the very best they could do was to suture the severed intestines and superficial wounds. Their efforts could only delay death and extend her agony. She retained consciousness as her pallid form endured to the numbing point the medication, scalpel, and needle. She repressed her groans and invoked Jesus, Mary, and her Babbo.

For two seemingly endless hours, while Assunta was immersed in prayer before the image of Mary in a niche in the corridor, Marietta's blood-drained flesh was wounded anew. Then it was over. As Marietta was removed from the operating room, she looked avidly for Assunta. She was taken to the tiny room devoted to the Madonna.

"Mamma dearest," the girl cried joyfully.

Assunta went to her bedside, kissed her with all the love of Heaven and earth, and asked, sadly, "How do you feel, my lovely child?"

"Good, Mamma!" Marietta said, cheerful in spite of her excruciating, life-stealing pain.

The doctors left Marietta in the care of the head of the infirmary, Donna Luisa Cuccalon de Bagner, and two Sisters of Poverty of St. Catherine of Siena, Srs. Beniamina and Aurelia. Assunta sat and held Marietta's pale hand, and her tears could not stop flowing.

"Mamma, why do you weep?" Marietta asked. "I ... I'm well!"

"Stay quiet, child. Do not force yourself to speak ... save your precious strength."

"Will you stay with me during the night?"

"It is not permitted, Marietta."

"Will we see each other in the morning, Mamma?"

"I live only for that, Marietta."

It was midnight, and the sisters motioned for Assunta to leave. She kissed her girl ardently and bathed her waxen face with her tears. When Assunta reached the doorway, Marietta turned and said with troubled concern, "And now where do you sleep, Mamma?"

"God will provide the place," Assunta responded.

"Good, Mamma," sighed Marietta, "that is the spirit, for Jesus answers all our needs ..."

Privation is the cup of the poor. Assunta had said that God would provide a lodging for her. She recalled the words of Jesus, "The foxes have holes, and the birds of the air have nests; but the Son of Man hath not where to lay his head."[8] In the dark stillness she saw the unhitched ambulance wagon in the stable yard. She went to it and stayed the remaining night hours within it.

She had not eaten since the frugal lunch her Marietta had prepared prior to the evil happening. Her soiled, ragged dress covered her work-strained limbs, for she had gone from gay threshing to deep tragedy. From the heat-laden ambulance, she stormed the gates of Heaven with pleadings for Marietta's life. It was not until a short time before the dawn of the Feast of the Most Precious Blood that she fell asleep.

The ringing of the church bells announcing the morning Mass awakened Assunta to the stark day of July 6. She roused herself and hastened into the hospital, to Marietta.

The child's untied blonde tresses were rich and shining upon the pillow and about her shoulders, her face was white and transparent. In the cool shades of the Madonna's little room, Marietta's expression was luminous.

Assunta kissed her burning forehead.

This child, the fruit of Christian union with Luigi, was unlike anyone she had ever known. Her goodness since birth, her lips never besmirched by unclean or contrary words, her understanding and cheer, her ever-giving and helping nature, her maternal compassion, her resolute virtue, her purity and devotion—all of these things filled Assunta's mind. Now death was tinting pale her beautiful Marietta, and it was obvious to Assunta that her child was above the fearsome angel; she was greater than the circumstance and act of the day before.

Assunta kissed her burning forehead. "How is my puppy this morning?" she whispered.

"Fairly well, Mamma," answered Marietta in a voice more enfeebled than the preceding night, "because today is the Feast of His Most Precious Blood. Mamma, where did you pass the night that seemed so long. O Mamma, I desire to see and embrace my brothers and sisters. But, Mamma, I beg you, do not let Alessandro come near me . . ."

Drs. Bartoli, Perotti, and Onesti came in to change Marietta's bandages and medicate her wounds. Her temperature had reached a fatal high, and from head to feet she was inflamed with fever. The doctors looked at each other and agreed she was beyond hope. Her life on earth would be a matter of a few hours at most.

Then the Carabinieri Ruggeri and Pierattini entered. The doctors advised them to keep their questioning of Marietta brief, as her life was surely ebbing.

In simple words, Marietta whisperingly related Alessandro's profane demand and, with her refusal, his merciless attack. At the request of Dr. Bartoli, Assunta asked Marietta if there had been other occasions when Alessandro had proposed evil.

Marietta calmly answered, "Yes, during the space of a month he had twice before approached me with sin ..."

"O sainted Mother of Christ!" exclaimed Assunta. "And why did you not tell me about this?"

Her eyes filling with tears, Marietta said, "Because Alessandro had vowed he would kill me if I told on him, and I believed him. With prayer and silence I hoped to disarm his intention. I thought perhaps he would soften and pity me, and not assault me. I prayed that the army might remove him from the house—from fear and shame I kept his threat to myself. But Alessandro has killed me just the same."

When the carabinieri had gone, Marietta said wanly, "I thirst, Mamma. Please do give me a drop of water."

Assunta looked pleadingly at the doctors. They shook their heads. They were fighting to save Marietta; water would only aid the deadly action of the peritonitis.

"Mariettina, the doctors have said that right now anything given you will cause further harm. Have patience for the love of Jesus, who on the Cross thirsted more than you."

At the remembrance of Jesus, Marietta tried to calm her need, but the crescendoing fire of her fever could not be calmed. "Give me a drop of water ... Is it possible that you cannot give me even one drop of water?"

But it was not with water that Marietta cooled her lips, but with her little metal crucifix, which she kissed tenderly, affectionately.

~ 8 ~

It was noon; the church bells were ringing again. They would toll once more that day, in mid-afternoon, when the statue of Jesus would be carried through the street in honor of the Feast of the Most Precious Blood. Fr. Martino brought her Holy Communion, the holy feast that only yesterday she had planned to attend with Teresa Cimarelli.

The priest sat by her and told her how Jesus rose above His terrible suffering to pray for His killers, pardoning them, excusing also the thieves at His side and promising them, "Today, shalt thou be with me in Paradise."[9]

He paused, then asked her, "Marietta, do you even pardon Alessandro Serenelli for the love you bear Jesus?"

Marietta gazed at her crucifix. She did not think of her young life crudely cut down but responded fervently, "Yes, of course, I forgive Alessandro. He did not know the evil he was doing. I forgive Alessandro and want him with me in Paradise."

The people keeping prayerful vigil in the corridor and outside the infirmary window overheard her words and echoed them with amazement and awe.

As Padre Martino held the Eucharist before Marietta he said, "Do you know what you are about to receive?"

"Yes," she answered weakly, smiling, "Jesus, whom I will shortly go to meet."

She opened her lips and took within her the Sacred Host. In the corner of the little room was a shrine of the Madonna. The early afternoon light from the window lighted the image.

"Please take me closer to the Mother of Heaven," Marietta begged. "I want to be by the Madonna."

Her bed was moved to Mary's side.

Assunta put her hands to her breast, bowed her head, and said, "Marietta, though I bore you, the Madonna is your true mother. Child of Heaven, His Mother is your Mother."

Often in her brief life, during the recital of the Rosary, Marietta had spoken the Ave Maria, and now she devoted the flickering last moments of her life, whispering, "*Ave, o Maria, piena di grazia; il Signore è con te. Tu sei benedetta* ..."

As tearful voices hailed Mary along with Marietta, their hearts cried, "Maria Goretti, stay with us!"

Srs. Beniamina and Aurelia brought in from the garden masses of roses and lilies in the name of the Most Precious Blood and placed them at the feet of the Madonna. Padre Martino bestowed a plenary indulgence on Marietta and said, "Little daughter, would it content you to have your name inscribed among the Daughters of Mary?"

"Oh ... much ... much!"

The priest placed around her neck a chain and medallion of the Congregation of the Daughters of Mary blessed at the church of San Pietro in Vinculis. It bore the invocation, "O Holy Mary, conceived without sin, pray for us." Marietta kissed the image fervently.

Then the child cried, "Mamma. Babbo is calling me." Assunta bit her lips and looked to the ground sadly.

"Forgive me, Mamma," Marietta said gently, "for reminding you of that sorrow too ..."

It was three o'clock, and the church bells sounded again. Dr. Bartoli whispered to Padre Martino, "Father, the hour of death is here."[10] Padre Martino sadly anointed Marietta's forehead with holy chrism and bestowed upon her the last sacrament. With the intoning of the Extreme Unction, a great sighing swept the people in the corridor and the crowd without.

Br. Meirado, the pharmacist of the hospital, bent to Marietta and said, "Maria, forget me not in Paradise."

Lucidly, she asked, "Who knows which of us will be permitted to enter first."

"You," cried the brother, "you certainly."

With a smile of humility, she responded, "Good ... if that is the way it is, I shall remember you there."

Marietta pressed her crucifix to her lips. Her eyes closed. It was as if a specter appeared before her, for she raised her arms defensively and with her final breath cried, "What are you doing, Alessandro? Your soul will go to Hell! No, Alessandro! Your soul is meant for Paradise ... I forgive you, Alessandro."

It was 3:45 in the afternoon on that July 6, 1902, that death fulfilled its errand.

On July 8, Marietta's funeral took place. Mourning thousands from Nettuno, Anzio, and even distant places came to the hospital chapel and filed tearfully past Marietta's bier. Though it was a work day, Nettuno's shops closed for the funeral.

Assunta was physically unable to attend the funeral. She did not see the long procession as it slowly moved through the streets toward the cemetery, nor the hushed reverence of the people who strew palms in the path of the horse-drawn hearse.

Maria was just a little peasant girl, poor and shabbily-dressed, but the crown of martyrdom was to be hers, and someday the whole Catholic world would love and venerate her, just as those thousands did then.

PART TWO

Repentance

For the grief that is according to God worketh repentance without regret, unto salvation.
—2 Corinthians 7:10

~ 1 ~

As he was being pulled with taut reins by the two mounted carabinieri along the scorching, dusty road to the Nettuno prison, Alessandro saw the despairing face of Assunta and even caught a glimpse of Marietta's prostrate form as the ambulance lurched by.

He had no remorse. He had dreamed of living like a jungle beast, and he had fulfilled that dream. He had dreamed of forcing his fate to change, and he had done so. He had shattered the dulling pattern of his life. "What difference does it make what happens to me," he thought. He believed in nothing, never had anything, and there was little for him to lose. Now his prison would have real walls he could touch. And now the authority he hated, which before had ignored him as if he did not exist, would have to reckon with his existence.

He remembered once, when he was a child in Torette, how on a noiseless, sweltering day a gentle ox suddenly bolted its yoke and gored the little girl who was leading it. The people of Torette had never forgotten that ox. Now he had broken his yoke, broken clear from the morass of nonentity. With the violence of his hands, he had changed himself from a nobody of a sharecropper's son, to a criminal whose name was on the tongues of many people.

They came to Nettuno. A crowd, curious and angry, filled the streets. They had waited to nightfall to see the attacker of the little peasant girl. Some watched the youth silently; others jeered him. There were cries that he was a beast and deserved lynching.

The carabinieri, fearful that the passions of the people might make them take vengeance in their own hands, hustled him through the streets to the primitive jail.

At first, Alessandro remained sullen under the questioning of the policemen. He refused to answer them or even to accept food. But about midnight, Carabiniere Ruggeri returned from the hospital and lied: "I have good news, Serenelli. You are fortunate, for Maria Goretti is not going to die. She will live, the doctors say. So your stubborn silence does not matter. Naturally, at the trial, she will tell the whole story, and you will not be able to deny it."

Alessandro still remained silent. In an understanding, fatherly voice, the carabiniere went on, "I was your age once and had the problem of bursting energy. I understand too well how these things occur. Everything will right itself. Maria Goretti will recover. You may stay in prison only a year, and then you can resume your normal life. Think of me as an older brother. Come, it will go easier for you if you confess all now."

Alessandro continued his adamant silence. Ruggeri rolled a cigarette and offered it to him.

"I do not smoke," Alessandro said.

"Will you join me in drinking a bottle of cool wine?"

Alessandro nodded.

As they drank, the carabiniere said confidentially, "Desire of the flesh is the very devil. Blinded by its spell, I would say we are only half guilty for what we do — in fact, the nature of life should share the other half of the blame. My people are peasants. As a young farmer, I was famished for a certain little peasant girl. But much water has run under the bridge since then. No man was meant to be an angel on this earth. You are a handsome fellow. Have you 'known' girls before?"

Alessandro vigorously shook his head.

"Ah. I see. Were you, are you, in love with Maria Goretti?"

"Love?" Alessandro echoed with surprise. "I have never known that sentiment, only desire."

"I understand. It is late. You cannot hide the facts forever. Will you tell all now?"

Alessandro hesitated for a moment, then answered, with a shrug, "Yes."

The carabiniere put his hand on Alessandro's shoulder and said sincerely, "This should not have happened. You should never have committed the act."

"What is done is done."

"I advise you as though you were of my own family: be careful of what you say. Try to help yourself. For your situation is bad enough as it is."

Alessandro responded with indifference, "What use have I to twist and color words when I care for nothing?"

Ruggeri called in two other carabinieri to write down and witness Alessandro's confession.

Alessandro said coldly, tersely:

"During the spring, thoroughly bored with a peasant's life—to the neck—I conceived a desire for Marietta that I had no reason to remove from my mind. I proposed my intention to her. She refused and from then on avoided me. That threw the fat into the fire. I determined that I would have her or kill her. Yesterday, I reached the end of my patience. I told myself that it had to be one way or the other. I would no longer bear frustration. When I pulled her into the kitchen, I threatened her with the brush hook to accommodate my desire or die. I did not expect her to resist me as furiously as she did.

"With her final refusal and outcry—that was it—I rained down hard blows with the brush hook upon her as though I were stripping corn or chopping wood. She fell, and I left her for dead, thinking surely that no one could survive such a hewing. Realizing escape from the open marshes was futile, I hid the brush hook behind the tool chest, locked myself in my room, cast myself upon the bed, and awaited the inevitable."

After Alessandro laboriously scrawled his signature to the confession, Ruggeri asked him, "Disgraced one, do you not have a word of regret? Are you not sorry for the terrible thing you did to little, fatherless Maria Goretti?"

Alessandro looked into Ruggeri's eyes and said clearly, "If Marietta had peacefully submitted to my desire, all would have been well. No one would have known otherwise. There would not have been this bother. Honestly, I would not have hurt a single hair of her head. But now, what is done cannot be undone."

In the morning, his father came, bringing to the jail shoes, trousers, a coat, some money, and the shirt Alessandro had ordered Maria to patch. Alessandro saw his father at a distance, stooped in deference, cap in hand, talking to the carabinieri. Giovanni's voice was quaking and cringing.

What good would a conversation with his father do, he asked himself. If he could not comfort the old man with lies, why should he add further stings of the truth that would be utterly strange to his comprehension? Could he say, "Father, why are you so pathetic? I did what seemed natural to my being. If you feel so badly, blame yourself and my mother for bringing me into the world."

Giovanni came toward the cell. He mumbled, "Alessandro, you were in a heat-struck fever yesterday and did not know what you were doing. Are you ill? Have you asked for a doctor?"

Alessandro thought, "How abject, how crushed is an old peasant when his son is taken for a crime by the police." Would his father understand that he had rebelled against everything and cared for nothing? No, and it was best not to pile incomprehensible words on the old man's misery, so he spoke very little.

On the way out, Giovanni said to Carabiniere Ruggeri, "My boy was without vices; he troubled no one; he read newspapers and magazines, and he was never given to temper. Alessandro was fond of Marietta, giving her his own copy of the *Christian Doctrine*, and on occasions defending her from my fault-finding." He shook his head in sorrow, the whole tragedy completely incomprehensible to him.

Before noon, Ruggeri returned from the hospital convinced by the doctors Maria Goretti could not possibly live. He thought it best to put Alessandro aboard the next train to Rome and send him to the Regina Coeli prison, for he feared the populace, learning of Maria's death, would react explosively and try to lynch Alessandro.

The railroad station was near the jail. As the carabinieri led the manacled Alessandro there, the crowds pressed about him. Though they felt hostile, the people of Nettuno wondered about him. In his suit, shirt, and shoes, shaven and with neatly combed hair, he was not the ugly beast they thought him, but a virile, contained youth, far handsomer than the average.

Aboard the train, Carabiniere Ruggeri told Alessandro, "The truth is as dark as it can be for you. Maria Goretti will be dead soon. The criminal court at Rome will try you for murder."

The train began to move, taking Alessandro away from the marshes he hated.

The Regina Coeli prison in Rome was the largest prison in Italy. Within the labyrinthine stone-beehive, he was assigned a small, narrow cell. Beneath the little, barred window was a cot with a hair mattress and, nearby, an open toilet.

The guard asked him if he knew how to read. Alessandro nodded. The guard then passed a paper through the bars to him.

"Here are the regulations for the detained. I advise you to read them carefully and obey the rules to the razor's cut. Otherwise, you will find yourself confined to a smaller cell."

That night was the second he was lying on a bed other than his own in the farmhouse at Le Ferriere. He used to lie in his bed planning the seduction of Maria, tossing and turning as he schemed the how and where of sensually taking her. Now he need no longer concern himself with that. He had decided that problem on the 5th of July. Now, in fact, there was no longer the responsibility of determining anything, for he was society's responsibility now. His revolt against toil, poverty, and frustration had been vanquished by society and religion's moral law, as proved and symbolized by Marietta's virtue. Let society see to him even as a defeated nation becomes the ward of the victor.

When he awoke in the morning, it took him moments to realize he was a prisoner in the very same Regina Coeli he had often read about in the crime stories. A guard came and passed a tin mug of water for drinking and washing to him. Later, the guard's cry of "authority" signified the hour when prisoners were permitted to receive lawyers and priests and have letters written for them. At eleven o'clock, he was given a small loaf of bread. At midday, the guard brought him a bowl of minestrone. And that was his allotted nourishment until the following morning.

~ 2 ~

On the morning of July 7, two days after the attack, the officials of the Palace of Justice, Cavaliere Vasso and Chancellor Lucchesi, went to Le Ferriere to gather the facts for the case against Alessandro.

In the Goretti farmhouse, they took note of that which spoke for itself: the gallery of magazine and newspaper pictures of enticing women and sensational criminals on the wall of Alessandro's room, and, but a few paces away, the blood, now dried, of little Maria.

The officials interrogated Assunta, Giovanni Serenelli, and the Cimarellis in Teresa Cimarelli's kitchen. Each told simply his part in the tragedy. Grief-stricken Assunta lovingly recalled the years of Maria's short life and her heroic spirituality, and she spoke of Alessandro without rancor. She showed the officials a copy of the *Christian Doctrine* Alessandro had given Maria to prepare for her First Communion. On its cover, the Madonna was instructing a little girl, and above the girl were two cherubim winging down to place a crown upon her head. Pressed with the pages of the booklet was a dried lily from Marietta's First Communion day, and on one of the pages was the charge, "Remember: Death rather than sin!"

The officials wanted the clothes Marietta was wearing at the time of the crime to exhibit as evidence in

Alessandro's trial. Assunta brought out and kissed the pierced, bloody bodice, petticoat, and skirt before parting with them.

The afternoon of the next day, in the Regina Coeli prison, Vasso and Lucchesi saw Alessandro. "Relate everything about your crime, before, during, and after," they ordered Alessandro. "Repeat exactly the version you gave to Carabiniere Ruggeri in the Nettuno jail."

Alessandro stolidly obeyed.

That afternoon, Alessandro was visited in his cell by two lawyers, Rossi and Canalintas.

"Serenelli, have you a lawyer?" Canalintas inquired.

Alessandro shook his head.

Then Rossi said, "Serenelli, we will represent you. All the newspapers are making much of your crime pro and con. You certainly have committed a big shocker. The story has gotten a rare notoriety throughout the land. This case has all the factors of a celebrated affair—an epic tragedy of the sharecroppers, with religion and society to blame. We will make this a famous case. We will do our best to get you off the hook with modified punishment, Serenelli."

Alessandro listened inattentively, indifferently, and when the lawyers left, he shrugged. He felt independent of the circumstances. What did the magnitude of his crime matter when suffering was the universal rule and not the exception for the peasant? He never had sought happiness, but did insist upon the certainty of the flesh. Deep within him, he was sullenly vexed with having derived little satisfaction from the way things turned out.

Three months later, on October 11, 1902, Alessandro was taken to the Court of Assize of Rome to stand trial for the murder of Maria Goretti.

Not yet twenty-one years of age and still a minor under Italian law, Alessandro was not placed in the caged dock but confined to the bench of the accused, flanked by two armed carabinieri attired in high prestige uniforms. The palatial court chamber was crowded. The Roman spectators had come to see a wild-eyed peasant, a beast, but were disappointed to find him a youth with regular features and restrained appearance.

Alessandro did not dare raise his eyes. Exposure to the view of the public was intolerable to him. He had read about that indefinable many-headed thing called "the people," the fickle sheep attracted to spectacles. And now, just as he had known about rapists and killers from newspapers, so did they know about him.

By his side was Lawyer Canalintas. In front of him was the lofty desk of the president of the court, Cavaliere Vitelli, in his magisterial hat and robes. To his right were the benches of the witnesses, and to his left was the jury box. On the witness benches were Count Mazzoleni, Cavaliere Marini, Carabinieri Ruggeri and Pierattini, the Cimarellis, Giovanni Serenelli—and Assunta Goretti.

After the jury was sworn in, the president said, "I have read thoroughly the report of the investigation and the confession of the accused. The case is clear. I advise the court to conclude this affair with dispatch."

The clerk read aloud the charge, Alessandro's confession, and the ghastly details of the autopsy report on Maria Goretti.

One by one, the witnesses were sworn in and testified. Their testimony confirmed the written findings. More imposing than the terrifying posture of the law was the peasant dignity of crushed Giovanni Serenelli, the Cimarellis, and Assunta Goretti. Assunta, shrouded in black shawl and dress, was a profoundly somber figure. Her strong, comely face, upright stance, sturdy shoulders, and muscular, calloused hands spoke of the strength won from hard toil of the earth.

Alessandro was summoned to the stand. He took the oath and answered the formal questions as to his name and date of birth.

The president commanded him to tell to the best of his ability the story of his crime.

Alessandro seemed puzzled by what was requested of him, then in all ingenuousness he stammered, "What I have done and said has already been written down on paper as fact. There is no need for me to talk."

"Those are matters for us to decide. It behooves the accused after he has confessed to repeat it during his trial in court for the records. Understand?"

Alessandro nodded respectfully. In a soft-spoken monotone, like a child reading from a primer, he told only the bare, explicit, non-philosophical structure of his crime, as if to mean: "Do I deny what I did? I tried to rape Marietta. She fought back. The natural heat of my desire then prompted me to kill her in reprisal for not being wanted. What more do you seek? You are the law. You are bigger than I. Do with me as you please. As for me, I am not concerned one way or the other."

Marietta's clothes were exhibited to him, and he was asked to identify the articles. "Yes," he nodded, without betraying feeling one way or the other, "that is the bodice and that is the particular skirt she was wearing when I went at her—the petticoat is not for me to know about."

The prosecutor presented him with the bloodstained brush hook.

"Alessandro Serenelli, do you recognize this object?"

"Of course I recognize it," responded Alessandro.

"This, then, is the weapon with which you struck Maria Goretti fourteen times?"

"Yes—but as for the number of times I struck it down upon Marietta—I did not make count."

"You sharpened this brush hook deliberately for your violent purpose—and the force of your blows bent the point!"

Alessandro shook his head. "Sir, allow me to say that is incorrect—to begin with, the brush hook belonged to the deceased Luigi Goretti but was in common use by all of us. It had last been sharpened by a youth who aided us with the farming. As for the point, it was twisted before I employed it upon Marietta."

The president said to Alessandro, "Prisoner at the bar, there is no doubt in the court's mind that you willfully killed twelve-year-old Maria Goretti when she resisted your sensual desire. What would you like to say in your defense?"

Alessandro remained silent. Finally the president added, "Young man, you must say something."

Alessandro answered in a low voice, "I have nothing to say. I said what I had to say with my first confession of the crime in the jail of Nettuno, and it was written down word for word."

"Do you consider that your defense?" asked the president.

"Defense?" echoed Alessandro with surprise. "No, Sir President, the truth."

Canalintas entered a plea for Alessandro in the liberal vein indigenous to the progressive currents of the times.

"Alessandro Serenelli's crime is distressing and humiliating to our concepts of what humanity should be, but at the same time, it casts a lurid light on our boasted civilization. Serenelli alone is not entirely culpable for his atrocious deed. Our vaunted authors who for profit have made passion and criminality intensely fascinating to the masses are equally guilty of Maria Goretti's death—also, organized religion with its impractical, uncompromising, unrealistic dictate: 'Death rather than sin!' Would it not have been better for all concerned if Serenelli were being charged with rape now rather than murder? The other two partners to Serenelli's crime are hereditary insanity—his mother and two brothers had disordered minds and died in mental institutions—and nature with its inexorable biological pressure.

"It is not fair to assume that this peasant youth could comprehend and cope with these potently determining and destructive factors impinging upon him.

"Along with the physically frenzied Serenelli who savagely struck down Maria Goretti, we must indict an inherited damaged brain, absence of a mother's love and guidance, the social phenomena of the widespread popularity of pornographic and horror literature, the mysticism and dogma of religion, and dispassionate nature's animal compulsion.

"Would it not be well for us to inquire, why does passion, capable of producing saints and heroes, so often direct the mentally incompetent to crime? The trial of Serenelli should be an example of a scientific exploration of the subject and the hidden secrets of good or evil.

"Our day and age creates crime by mental contagion through its newspapers, novels, and magazines, and even our stage portrays wholesale butchery which we applaud. Our literature copies crime—the crime of passionate outbreaks—just as crime of the same type in turn copies literature.

"With awkward ability to read, Alessandro Serenelli absorbed into his limited and inflexible peasant mind the crimes daily glamorized by literature, between the lines of which is the subliminal suggestion, 'Go you and do likewise.' Our literature, which publicizes and glorifies by indirection passion and crime, is a school of sensuality, teaching the ever pernicious lesson that crime is justified as flowing from an overmastering emotion."

Canalintas asked the court for adjournment of the trial, with the hope that the jury would reflect favorably upon his plea and extend a leniency of punishment with the inevitable sentencing of Alessandro.

President Vitelli adjourned the trial to the day after the following day, October 13. To the members of the jury he admonished, "I wish the jury to bear in mind and beware of the sensationalistic and undue influence of sophistries the counsel for defense sees fit to exercise. Remember, literature is one thing, and the Criminal Assizes is another."[11]

Lawyer Canalintas visited Alessandro in his cell.

"Listen young man, if you do not help me to prove that you were not in possession of sanity when you attacked the

Goretti girl, it will go severely with you. I will also try to establish circumstances of provocation you were subjected to. It might soften the court to lighten your punishment."

"I cannot seem to be interested in all that now," said Alessandro. "I knew beforehand what I might do, one way or the other. I know what I did and why."

Canalintas threw up his hands. "If you insist upon thwarting my efforts to help you with your *truth*, you will receive the maximum sentence of thirty years—and if you were twenty-one, you would be condemned to life imprisonment. Very well!"[12]

Dr. Giovanni Mingazzini, the director of the Lungara hospital of psychiatry, came to Alessandro's cell.

Canalintas asked him, "What have you come here for?"

Mingazzini answered authoritatively, "The court has sent me to do that which you do not know how to do!"

Canalintas took Alessandro aside. "He is going to give you a mental examination. If you let him find you sane, I will have wasted my time in this case!"

Mingazzini examined Alessandro for hours, putting him through various tests such as distinguishing coins and bills as well as colors and related objects, having him read from newspapers, and asking him many questions.

He found Alessandro's mental capacity to be somewhat above the peasant level and saw that Alessandro was proud of his intelligence, and he encouraged Alessandro to candidly state his opinion of himself, his life, and his crime.

Alessandro expressed himself without nervousness in a matter of fact manner. "Maria Goretti did not lend cause to my desire or lead me on in any way. Apprised of my intention, she did her best to not let it come about. She was a little girl good and pure. That drew me.

"I was bored, and stung by a life of exhausting labor and hopeless bondage to landowners, and so I reasoned that it made no difference if I did commit a crime and was incarcerated. The idea came to me especially when reading about great criminal acts in the newspaper *The Messenger*, and I said to myself each day, 'I should break the law too!' Without delusion or insanity, I decided to have Marietta or kill her."

"Do you have remorse now for having killed Maria Goretti?"

After a long silence, Alessandro said, "If Marietta had peacefully obeyed me and submitted to my desire, I would not have given her the slightest hurt."

Dr. Mingazzini concluded his notes with the decision that, "The accused, Alessandro Serenelli, is sane of mind."

On October 13, despite attempts by Canalintas to prolong the trial, the jury swiftly found Alessandro guilty of the murder of Maria Goretti.

On October 15, Alessandro stood before the prisoner's bar to receive his sentence. President Vitelli declared, "The Court of Assizes judges that the motive of the guilty condemned, Alessandro Serenelli, was to abuse the trust of domestic relations within his father's and the Goretti family's household, and to willfully outrage the purity of the little girl Maria Goretti with voluntary premeditation to facilitate the consummation of the crimes of rape with the alternative of murder or both.

"The court judges that Alessandro Serenelli, at the moment of committing the crime for which he has been found guilty, was not affected with any form of neuropsychopathy, but had instead full consciousness and liberty of his actions. He was completely responsible for the murder of Maria Goretti. Therefore the court in view of that fact believes it just to deal out the maximum punishment prescribed by the law.

"Alessandro Serenelli, the court condemns you to thirty years imprisonment to be served in the following manner: first, three years in solitary confinement, and the other twenty-seven years at hard labor."

The president asked Assunta Goretti if she had any final words to utter as the mother of Alessandro's victim. Assunta arose, gazed upon Alessandro with Christian pity, and answered, "Yes, Sir President — I forgive Alessandro!"

A wave of silence came over the courtroom, then many, recovering from the astonishment created by Assunta's charity, cried out indignantly, "Never!" "It should not be!" "I would never forgive him!"

Assunta quickly faced those who had raised their voices, and asked, "And suppose in turn, Jesus Christ does not forgive us?"

~ 3 ~

ASSUNTA AND GIOVANNI Serenelli returned to the land. Obligation to the earth and to the landowner could not be interfered with, even by tragedy. The contract with Count Mazzoleni had to be honored. The landowner's interest took precedence over the joys and woes of his peasants.

With the November grain in, the ultimate harvest of the migration in search of bread for the Gorettis and Serenellis could be summed up thus: Luigi Goretti and Maria dead and buried; the virtuous image of Marietta already taken up and claimed by religious youth groups; Alessandro Serenelli sentenced to thirty years in prison; and Assunta with five children on her hands, more destitute than ever.

Giovanni Serenelli left the Le Ferriere farmhouse with a dull curse in his heart for it and the polluted marshes, to labor again in the stony fields of Torrette near Corinaldo. Behind his back, he was pointed out as the misery-laden father of that youth who killed that saint-like girl.

One raw, December morning, Assunta walked to the separate graves of her husband and daughter, fell down upon them, and kissed the earth covering them. Then, she bundled up her five children, tendered her gratitude to the Cimarellis, and, with trainfare donated by charitable neighbors, returned to her home village of Corinaldo. There she found only an abandoned stable in which to shelter her family, the crucifix, and the picture of the Madonna. There she began the seemingly endless struggle to exist. She toiled in the sparse fields and did the meanest work in other people's homes; her children begged their bread in the public square.

In Rome, Lawyer Canalintas visited Alessandro once more and told him, "The law allows me to appeal your case within three days, but by your unrepentant confession, and the way you answered questions before and during the trial, it seemed you were perversely anxious for your own doom, practically stating you had a natural right to violate a little girl's morals and take her life. I fear if I appeal the case, with your attitude and testimony, it might end all the worse for you — with perhaps six years solitary confinement, instead of the three you already have to serve."

Without any expression on his face, Alessandro said, "I have no taste to be dragged back into court. I have had my bellyful. What is there to bother about? I did what I wanted to do — what I had to do. As I told myself before my deed of July 5, these things would go, as they say, either to the right hand or to the left hand — and I was not unaware of the possible consequences, believe me. I feel now that we should let bad enough alone. I respectfully thank you for what you have tried to do for me. All in all, I did change the mode of my life."

On October 18, Alessandro was to begin his three years of solitary confinement. A prisoner in the adjoining cell asked him, "Have you any idea what that means?"

"So I will be by myself. What else is there to it?"

"You will soon learn what there is to it!" the prisoner replied.

From October 18 on, he was completely segregated from the other prisoners in a cell closed off except for a small, barred window and a square slot in the solid door. During the daylight hours, he was given work: the gluing together of match boxes. He could make twenty boxes an hour, and for every thousand, he was paid twenty cents.

Minutes, hours, days moved spitefully slow. There was the stone ceiling, floor, and four walls, the mocking, tiny, barred window, the cot, the open toilet and its squalor, the clay food bowl, tin water mug, the stack of cardboard pieces and the glue pot for the match boxes, the fleeting moments when the guard's face appeared at the door-slot. He tried to do away with thinking, and did, for a time. Yet for how long during the thirty years before him could he pretend to maintain an arid interior? If he could only fall asleep and awaken in 1932!

During February came a few days respite from the obscure torment of solitary confinement. He and five other convicts were to be sent to their designated permanent prison at Noto on the island of Sicily.

Three carabinieri escorted them. Alessandro was the youngest of the prisoners. He had the shaven head, the iron handcuffs, and coarse, woolen brown and green striped suit of the convict. Some passengers on the train recognized him from the newspaper photos. His companions were thieves and murderers. The prisoners made the most of the trip, asking for cigarettes from passengers saddened by their misfortunate plight, singing, joking with the carabinieri, and carrying on as though they were on a holiday excursion.

At the Naples station, there was an overnight wait for the train south. With the permission of the carabinieri, a solicitous Neapolitan offered to fetch wine. Alessandro, not wishing to be obviously different, contributed a dollar from his meager purse. The convicts waited in vain for the Neapolitan to return. As the train pulled out of Naples, Alessandro said philosophically, "The Neapolitan has drunk our wine to our health."

The train ran along the Mediterranean coast for hundreds of miles, close to the water's edge. The soothing sight of the vast green sea revived memories of another time—the five years he enjoyed on the boats among the pagan fishermen. The convicts frankly voiced their dreams of being rid of the handcuffs and carabinieri and of being footloose aboard the ship on the horizon. Alessandro said nothing. What was to be, was to be. He was a remorseless recluse in the solid structure of his flesh, and it was no use to attempt to be otherwise.

Then each fell to airing his crime. Mancini, a thirty-year-old goldsmith, had murdered two wives for insurance money. He was trapped after committing the second crime. A Piedmontese,[13] schooled in stealing since childhood, tried to pick the pocket of a sleeping man aboard a train; the man awoke, pulled out a pistol; the Piedmontese wrested the pistol from him and shot his intended victim. Turning to Alessandro, he commented, "I did that which is contrary to the art of my trade—a thief should steal, not kill. How long will you be a guest of the government?"

"Thirty years," answered Alessandro.

"Ah, the maximum for your age. Whatever you did, you went the whole way. What did you do?"

Alessandro was silent for a spell, and then said, "I am a principal in the Goretti-Serenelli case."

"And what was that about?"

"Is it possible you heard no talk about my crime in the area of the Pontine Marshes—Le Ferriere, to be exact? The newspapers made much of it!"

At Reggio, the convict group was ferried across the Strait to Messina. Gilberto, the friendliest of the carabinieri, said to Alessandro as the train left for Noto, "You are now outside of the continent. Usages and customs are different here. Considering that you will have to spend your youth and the better part of your life in Noto, you might as well look to Sicily as a second fatherland. In and around the prison, you will find the Sicilians quick to wrath and blows, and peculiarly fanatic about religion, but warm and human. Do as you are commanded; forget time, expiate your crime, and with God's will, someday you may be a free, older, and wiser Christian."

On this terminating stretch of his journey, Alessandro took in avidly the last glimpses of the world beyond the Noto prison walls that awaited him. There was the smoking volcano of Etna, lava slopes that looked like the Hell of Dante, the steep coast that jutted perilously over the Ionian Sea, the yellowed terrain of the sulfur mines, clay plains shaggy with blackened stubble and clumps of caper and licorice, and circling ravens; on isolated roads here and there were high-wheeled, brightly painted donkey carts; on the hillsides were tall, dark poplars; in village streets were the prized milk-giving Maltese goats; between Catania and Siracusa were fields of flowering almond blossoms, lemon and orange trees, vineyards, groves of wild, low palms, and on steep terraces overlooking the purple and violet sea were groves of olive trees whose leaves gleamed silver in the sun-washed light. Beholding the quiet, natural wonders, Alessandro almost forgot he was a murderer.

The ancient city of Noto seemed not in Italy but in a place in Asia with its Saracen and Byzantine architecture.[14] The old prison was on an esplanade in the center of the city. Visible through the high gates was the mother church of Noto nearby which contained the corpse of Noto's patron saint, San Corrado Confalonieri.

Alessandro's cell was smaller and darker than that of the Regina Coeli prison.

~ 4 ~

IN THE SOLITARY confinement block, each prisoner in his dismal cell was assigned the task of making cord and weaving fibers out of palm leaves. The lengthy, thorny wild palm leaves were raked through with a large, wooden-backed comb bearing three rows of sharp, iron teeth. There were nine knife-like teeth to a row. The guard came into each cell three times a day to count the teeth of the instrument.

"I never know," said Picardi, one guard, "when one of you in desperation decides to kill himself and cause me to lose my job."

At first, Alessandro tried resisting the ponderous loneliness by singing, "Serenelli, cheerful be, after twenty-nine years and six months, you and I will be free!" But the sound of his own voice was unconvincing and echoed uselessly to his hearing. Life was a condition that had to release the gift of strength, the vital force that constituted being, and had to absorb in turn the rays not only of planets but also that of fellow humans, those potent emanations not seen but felt. Sitting or standing, the ten hours a day he ripped and combed through the prickly palms and piled up mounds of hempen fibers allowed his hands to speak their physical language. It was when daylight left the high, tiny window that aloneness surrounded him maddeningly. There was a furrow in the stone pavement from the cot to the cell door worn down by other inmates before him. And in that track of restlessness and impatience he paced interminably back and forth the sluggish hours of the extended nights "like the wolf of Rome" or "the pilgrims circling forever the Blessed House of Loreto."[15]

Exhaustion would eventually bring on meager sleep, but in his slumber there was never a dream, a respite and flight from reality, and upon waking it was as though he had not slept and that the nerve-drumming silence and suffocating loneliness had never been interrupted.

Being alive became the outstanding frustration. He could not explain to the parts of his physical life that they had to be constrained to a tight cell until 1905, and after, detained twenty-seven years more within limited, walled grounds. How could the mind justify to consciousness and restless flesh that they had to vegetate and age for three decades in prison? Often he desperately felt that death or madness would be the path of escape from the intolerable burden of solitary confinement, but the thought of stabbing himself, hanging, and picturing himself an inert corpse, or being deprived of his mental faculties, repelled him shudderingly. Then again, why lose his mind or kill himself and give his nemesis, society, that satisfaction?

Once a year he received a letter from his sister-in-law Maria, the wife of his brother Pietro in Torrette, telling him of his crushed, old father Giovanni and about themselves, and enclosing a few dollars. With the ending of the first letter she had said, "Have patience, Alessandro. Do not blame others for your fate. You yourself blindly swung the pickaxe into your own feet."

On October 18, 1905, he was let out of confinement and put in the lively collective section among three hundred prisoners. At last he had emerged from a nether world, a world of mute, choking shades, a solitariness of underground darkness, like a human mushroom brought to the light of day from out of bioluminescent gloom.

He complimented himself for having survived the terrible aloneness and inquired how others had fared in solitary during his three years. He learned that three had killed themselves, six had gone mad and were removed to the insane asylum, and a few who had endured the confinement, when released, cracked and committed suicide.

When assigned to cobbling, he refused to obey, claiming that by nature he had always been hostile to sedentary work. For his disobedience he was put in stocks for ten days. After a period of sedentary tasks, he was sent out to labor in the great, open courtyard, to turn the large, horizontal, wooden wheel that was used to weave the dried palm fibers into cord.

His heart was still resentful and cynical. For three years he turned the weaving wheel, and cursed man and Heaven. He listened to the others talk about their crimes. Some had successfully violated girls without being apprehended, and there were also stories of men in high places who had done the same. Yes, in every man lurked the possible rapist and killer. If, fearing the shame of the violation being known or to save her life, the girl acquiesces, the sensual man is then not included in the public criminal ranks. Supposing he had been a Mazzoleni or one of the wealthy ruling class? One never or rarely heard of the rich and powerful being punished for an act of passion. Before his crime he thought the world repressed him beyond all reason; now his body was caged, trapped by society, and he was infinitely worse off.

If Marietta had submitted, he would have made a habit of it. That was six years ago. Requited desire would surely have brought about a change of his feelings toward the world. Sooner or later she would have become the mother of his child—a not uncommon happening amongst the peasants and the poor. Assunta was a tractable and natural woman—there would not have been any trouble—none of society's business—a situation would have discreetly been settled between the Gorettis and the Serenellis—he would have married Marietta and perhaps developed a sentiment for her also.

Was not her stubbornness as mad as his desire? Her fanatic refusal. See what it had led to? If she had only submitted—if! And thus with each useless, wasted, senseless, dragging day within the prison walls, bitterness gnawed him.

It was five in the morning, December 28, 1908. A great, continuing earthshock trembled his cell and split open the thick, stone walls; the floor heaved, the barred window and the cell bars twisted. The hundreds of prisoners cried with fright. The guards ran through the corridors, opening the cell doors and shouting, "Calm yourselves! Everybody file out into the courtyard!"

Alessandro huddled with the other prisoners in the courtyard away from the cracking, falling walls as shock after shock rumbled the ground.

For two days and nights, as the earthquake vent its fury, the religious amongst both the prisoners and their keepers prayed for succor to Noto's patron, St. Corrado. The news came that Messina, not too distant from Noto, caught by the full brunt of the earthquake and tidal waves, had been wiped out in thirty-two seconds with a loss of seventy thousand lives.

One of the convicts said to Alessandro, "Enough innocent Christians to fill Rome's vast Colosseum have been mashed to bits in Messina in the twinkling of an eye, and we killers, brigands, and men of evil in prison have not been scratched. Here we are alive—well, thank God for that!"

One night, soon after the earthquake, a dream came to him. The dream was so vivid he could not distinguish it from reality.

The prison bars and walls fell away, and his cell was a sunlit garden blooming with flowers. Toward him came a beautiful girl dressed in pure white. He said to himself, "How is this; peasant girls wear darkish clothes?" But he saw it was Marietta. She was walking among flowers toward him, smiling, and without the least fear. He wanted to flee from her but could not. Marietta picked white lilies and handed them to him saying, "Alessandro, take them." He accepted the lilies one by one, fourteen of them. But a strange thing took place. As he received them from her fingers, the lilies did not remain lilies but changed into so many splendid, flaming lights. There was a lily turned to purifying flame for every one of the fourteen mortal blows he struck her on the fatal day in Le Ferriere. Marietta said smilingly, "Alessandro, as I have promised, your soul shall someday reach me in Heaven." Contentment entered his breast. And the scene of incredible beauty dissolved in silence.

When he awoke, it seemed that the rabid, choking, consuming feelings of hate, destruction, and bitterness that ruled within him were loosening their invisible bonds from his mind and flesh.

Alessandro changed after that. A sensation of the positive value of the spirit related to life slowly began to permeate him. The quantities of space and time were then changing for him and becoming different. The bare cell, restricted grounds, and walls no longer seemed relentless hands clutching his throat, and time, instead of ceaselessly whipping him into despair, commenced to assume a tolerable rhythm. An interest in his labor, and people and things other than himself, healthily came into his ken. The transformation began immediately after the dream of Marietta. Or was it a dream? But how could he dare suppose it was more than a dream? In the new light he now saw the full horror of what he had done to Marietta. How could he possibly deserve the salving visitation from her? Were there to be extraordinary, mystic results from his cruel and merciless crime upon a good little girl? Like the calm surface of the sea shattered by a violent stone, and then the ripples instead of fading away, enlarging to ever-expanding circles reaching beyond earthly life? He had never dreamed in his sleep. He had not conjured that dream of Marietta coming to him, the dream of beautiful significance that he could never have imagined himself. Why, following the dream, did life and spirit suddenly and for the first time ever appear precious to him? Was Marietta chosen for a destiny that transcended her death?

No, it could not be for him to answer. All he knew was that the dream of Marietta relaxed his awful tension, opened the gate of his interior world, and came as a harbinger of a peace he had never experienced.

He was removed from the turning of the wheel and the cord weaving and sent to work in the laundry. Prisoners who had long taken him for a sullen loner were surprised to see him newly cheerful and cooperative. He was accepted as a friend during the group conversations and learned about those working with him. One, an Abruzzian,[16] said, "Returning from a trip, I saw my betrothed dancing with a stranger at a party. In a fit of jealousy I picked up an iron chair and brained her. Now, for the rest of my life to think about it, I ask, why do we kill women, without whom the human race would end?"

There was Pambianchi, a likeable fellow, who would say, "I should have heeded my mother who told me, 'My son, learn to appreciate honest labor, for the trade of the thief brings him to an ugly pass.'"

Some boasted of their crimes, and many claimed that they had been framed for a crime someone else had committed. The convict, Canepina, told Alessandro his story: "I was taught to kill as a soldier in Africa. I did more than my share and killed many, for which I received medals. I completed my army service and come back to my hometown a hero. Then, as a civilian, I had occasion to kill a man over a game of cards. It seems impossible now that I have to spend the rest of my life in prison for only one killing!"

During a free period and chatter in the prison yard, a fierce, Sardinian matricide, who had recently come from five years of solitary confinement and got to know Alessandro in the laundry, said, "Serenelli, they say for six years you were bitter and unfriendly. Now you seem at home. How do you adjust yourself to rot for thirty years, the prime years of your life, in prison?"

Hesitantly, Alessandro related his dream of Marietta and said that since then his poisonous, evil feelings against the world were leaving him.

The prisoners listening were awed by his dream. The Sardinian, a deeply religious man, nodded. "The soul of the girl you slew came to you in that dream with the message that she seeks to save you. She wants to be your intercessor. You are fortunate, Serenelli, and will be saved.

"My mother betrayed my father with his own brother. I caught them, and for my father's honor I stabbed them to death. What I did should not have been the concern of the law. Your dream of the Goretti girl is a sign of salvation. But I am damned from the other world; I dream of my wretched mother every night; she pursues me to destroy me. There is no saint in Heaven helping me."

One morning, a few weeks later, the guards found the Sardinian dead, hanging from a piece of the prison-made cord.

~ 5 ~

ONE AFTERNOON IN the autumn of 1910, while Alessandro was at the laundry scrub-board, the guard said to him, "Go to the cortile. The Bishop of Noto has come to visit you." On a bench in the sunlit cortile was venerable old Bishop Giovanni Blandini. Alessandro wondered, why would the high prelate come to visit the murderer of a little girl? As he approached the bishop, he trembled and halted with painful shame. The bishop kindly beckoned to him to sit by his side.

The aged bishop had a golden cross upon his breast, and in his hands a small book. His penetrating and compassionate eyes studied Alessandro.

"My son, do you recall Cavaliere Marini from the days of Le Ferriere?"

"Yes, your Excellency. He was a most Christian man and sympathetic to the hard lot of us peasants."

"Since the people of the land, like streams running to the sea, seek the spirit of Maria Goretti in their prayers and devotions, Cavaliere Marini has been inspired to write her story. He and Bishop Tito Cucchi of Senigallia have written me to visit you and ascertain the state of your soul."

The sweet, mild voice of the bishop spoke of Christ, who does not deny even to the very worst sinners His light of commiseration, forgiveness, and the hope for a new day. "The way of man passes, but the soul brought to light lives forever. Society punishes. Christ saves. Marietta knew and tried to tell you. Alessandro, if you accept the love of Christ reaching out to you, you will be reborn a truly Christian soul. Do not fight the Lord; surrender to Him and become the Alessandro Serenelli He wishes you to be, as Marietta Goretti so wanted for your sake."

Gentle love was being offered him. And he had kept himself from loving anyone. He had always thought that hatred was his proper dwelling. Hatred of the world had magnified his sensual desire and made him kill a girl who was as a little sister to him. It was clear to him now that her virtue was stronger than his hatred. He had been monstrously wrong. It was because of Marietta's worth that the bishop came to him in prison with Christ's love. His heart swelled and new words came from his mouth.

"I want to cast myself upon God's mercy. I want to beg pardon from the family of her whom I destroyed. I want to go on hands and knees before Assunta Goretti and her children for what I have done."

"If you are sincere, tell it to me in a letter."

"I write but poorly."

"Simple words coming from your soul will suffice."

As the bishop was leaving, Alessandro falteringly asked, "Your Excellency, may I be permitted to read the story of Maria Goretti?"

The bishop handed him the booklet and blessed him.

That night, by candlelight in his cell, he read Marini's book. Every word was a salutary piercing of his new-found soul. He was returned to the scene of Le Ferriere to behold the Serenellis and Gorettis. He saw them toil the marshes and sweat and ache with fatigue, and he realized the plain goodness of the Goretti husband and wife and again received their kindnesses.

He heard the dying Luigi Goretti tell Assunta to return to Corinaldo as the Serenellis bear the portent of evil. He watched the Marietta of innocence and sacrifice take over the burden of the household, and he shrank as the repressed, misguided Alessandro planned to seduce her. Was this he who accosted her profanely in the field? It was torturous beyond description for him to read in detail how this other young Alessandro, who was himself, judged that Marietta must be either seduced or destroyed, and how, on the broiling summer afternoon, he rushed along on an inexorable track to rape and, when justly resisted, to mortally hack Marietta down into life-dripping pools of blood. The book repeats her words, "Alessandro, I forgive you — I want your soul with mine in Paradise!" Her cry reverberated through the years. Now at last, at the age of twenty-eight, a cloudburst of tears rained down upon the parched, acid desert of his being. If only he could go back to July 5, 1902, and strike off the mad hands of his former self! His eyes, which had never known weeping, were now floodgates spilling ceaseless, scalding tears upon each page of the story of Maria Goretti. Ferocious and cold had been his evil other self, but now implacable was his remorse, and in anguish he kissed again and again the artist-drawn likeness of Marietta.

Was it Cavaliere Marini's interpretation of the tragedy and suggestion of Marietta's probable sanctity that was causing this purifying emotion within him? No, no, not the printed word of an author's own thoughts but a spiritual power gave him new, clear eyes and revealed to him his eternal soul, showing that behind in the past was the nightmare of the unbeliever, the killer Alessandro. He felt, he knew, and told himself that the force transforming him could be no other than the spirit of little Marietta.

With aid from the Abruzzean convict in the next cell, he wrote the following ornate letter to Bishop Blandini of Noto:

> Most Reverend Excellency,
>
> I cannot sufficiently express the comfort my grieved being received from the honor of the colloquy with your illustrious Excellency; for which I send you my gratitude without measure. If it be true that in a strangely fated moment of mental aberration I was constrained (that is, impelled by passion beyond my control) to do an act of barbarous homicide, for which the law has already meted to me accorded punishment, I cannot fully accuse myself unconditionally and say that my act was solely and voluntarily for the purpose of doing so great an evil, because my green age and my meager cognizance of mature life were the real causes for bringing me to the sorry pass that today I bitterly weep over. Multiplied is my weeping, for now my grown conscience tells me I have bereft the life of a poor innocent who until the tragic end wished to save and maintain her virginal honor, sacrificing herself to a brutal death rather

than to my desire, all of which fact has spun me into the terrible abyss. I publicly detest my crime and ask forgiveness from God and also from the poor and desolate family of my victim. I want to hope that even I am able to obtain forgiveness like so many others on this earth. To your excellency I present the declaration of the hope that even you will forgive me for the major evil done by the inexpert youth I was, and that your prayers may unite with mine to ask forgiveness for me from Him who governs all, and may I receive a calm sea and benediction with my poor final extinction.

I respectfully kiss your hand and beg from you a feeling of forgiveness.

—Alessandro Serenelli

For Alessandro, the element of time metamorphosed into a reasonable entity, an amenable concept, leniently distributed from day to day between bodily requirements met, the work in the laundry, religious services, friendly relations with the guards, chaplain, warden, the fellow convicts about him, the reading of good books in his cell, and dreamless sleep.

As out in free society, so in the prison of Noto there were all gradations of mankind: harsh and sadistic guards, kind and understanding guards, prisoners who had to fight and kill each other, the utterly depraved, the perverts, the illiterate, the educated, the sensitive, the bestial, the gentle, the corrigible, and the hopelessly incorrigible.

He was determined to stay away from trouble and serve his entire sentence in peace. Being his own enemy had landed him in jail; if he had not listened to his own impulsive dictates and had routinely obeyed the commonplace hard and fast rules of Church and law, he would not be in prison. What use was the path of rebellion when it made one a fish only to be hooked by the throat? What did it profit a man to indulge in fancy and hurt himself? He turned his back on the ugly and stark happenings between the convicts. Whatever they did was their own business. Many of the inmates spoke of loved ones, wives, children, sweethearts, and what they intended to do when freed. He did not dare to anticipate the future. Would he live to be out in the world again? But why should he dream and wonder or excite himself about anything? See what his youth and the world had done to him. Let others smash their heads against the why and wherefore of life; for him, it would be easier to float with the inexplicable mass flow of time as an orderly microscopic person, not interfering in the course of any other human being.

The days accumulated smoothly into years. He enjoyed small pleasures such as the gifts of food brought into the prison on holy feast days by the townspeople and the wife of the guard Picari. Picari said once, "Look, Alessandro, my wife brings me ordinary dry spaghetti but sends you pasta seasoned with chicken sauce. She treats a convict better than she does her own husband!"

The three special holidays of the year were Christmas, Easter, and the feast in September of Noto's patron, St. Corrado. The fiery-tempered Sicilians were unusually religious and very charitable to the prisoners of Noto. Quite often, a wealthy farmer would bring a calf into the Church of St. Corrado, have the priest bless it, then butcher the animal and donate it to the kitchen of Noto's prison. The warden, Corrado Ficcavento, a native of Noto, was a kindhearted and paternal man, and his wife was also interested herself in the welfare of the prisoners. On feast days, the warden saw to it that his wards had double portions of bread, a meat dish, and a bottle of wine made from luscious grapes of his own vineyard.

Sunday mornings, Alessandro always attended the Mass celebrated by the chaplain, Don Michele, at a portable altar in the mess hall. The days when he drew back from the thought of faith and religious practice had long since dissolved away. Why should he not immerse himself in the serenity of belief? Though with the ceremonies he was not capable of the rare mystic and passionate rapport with the invisible God, he gave himself unquestioningly, submissively, to confession, the Mass, Communion, and prayer. All but his prayers to Marietta had a general, ritualistic form. His prayers to Marietta were offered directly. His simple invocations were addressed to her personally as though she were near to him as she had been in Le Ferriere. Traditional doctrine told of Heaven's hosts whom one met after death, but he had known Marietta in life; the child had been under the same roof with him for three years or more; she and her goodness had been as substantially real to his knowing as the earth of the fields. The Son of God forgave His killers, and Marietta forgave him as he was killing her. Intense, soul-shriving, nightly were his prayers to her.

~ 6 ~

HE BECAME A model prisoner, working efficiently in the laundry, turning the other cheek to any offenses sent his way, keeping his person and cell clean, helping others, volunteering for unpleasant tasks, refraining from complaint and blasphemy, and conscientiously avoiding the least infraction of prison regulations.

The chaplain was fond of him and interested in his predilection for reading. Don Michele, a bit senile, playing the national lottery for a few pennies a day, was a highly educated man of letters. He brought Alessandro books of the great authors from his private library. Once a week he opened the wicket of Alessandro's cell door and would say, "Did you finish the last book? I brought you another good one."

At night, while fellow prisoners sang, chattered, cursed, snored, mooned, or restlessly paced about their cells, Alessandro sat or lay on his cot and read by candlelight. Reading had been Alessandro's earliest and only pleasure. In Noto, he returned to that realm which led imagination magically beyond the prison walls. It was ironic that the compelling reading habit that fanned the fire toward his crime in the Le Ferriere farmhouse now was a wall of solace and his intimate and richly rewarding friend. He realized the fact that the printed word could be a potent influence for the activation of either good or evil. It was like a substance taken into one's being;

putrid air or poisonous food made for illness and even death; the consummation of profound and humanistic letters evoked healthy, compassionate feelings for life. At night his cell was the protected privacy, his study, schoolroom, and world-stage; at night he was not a prisoner.

At night the faults of self, the trammels of reality, did not exist. Book in hand, by the flicker of the candle, he was the witness, guest, confidant of the Evangelists, Goethe, Dumas, Dante, Manzoni, Bertoldo, Pellico, Dostoevsky, Tolstoy. He read slowly, and with peasant tenacity went over and over the difficult passages. He had an instinct for the dramatic elements, and, when moved by a tragic or illuminating phrase or situation, would read it aloud to enjoy the sounding out of the words. Reading could hurt him no more as it did at Le Ferriere; literature had become his silent, obedient, and revealing companion. The scenes and ideas he absorbed he now knew he was to marvel at and not ever transfer into physical expression.

Often, a fellow prisoner would comment, "Alessandro, you never say much." He would nod and smile. With the vast amount of good reading, learning anew and differently each night of lives that he safely entered, lived with, and left, he somewhat understood his habitual reluctance for speech. During the prison day, the others uselessly and interminably repeated what they had said before. Why should he imitate the talkers and irritate time with unconstructive words?

Books that contained characters who sinned greatly, were punished by law and conscience, and who after long sufferings finally found redemption, were particularly dear to him. He was impressed by *The Betrothed* by Manzoni because the murderous brigand of the hills received grace and reformed into a holy man. *Faust* he reread many times, feeling pity for a character who deliberately sold his soul to the devil.

The one book that fascinated him most strongly and which he tremblingly reread with a poignant sense of his own bloody guilt was *Crime and Punishment*.[17] He understood only too well Raskolnikov's stream of consciousness and criminal premeditation. He shuddered as the anti-social, raging young man hacked his victim. And every time he reached the end of the book, he wept with joy for the killer's remorse and salvation. The return to reading was now to become a permanent habit never again to be interrupted. Once more, but harmlessly and for the better, the world of reading was more satisfying and real than actual life.

One day in December, 1910, Don Michele handed him a newspaper article to read and said, "My son, you should see this, if only for the increased fervor of your penitential devotions."

The article described the celebration of the feast of the Immaculate Conception at the Vatican where in his homily Pope Pius X warmly eulogized Maria Goretti as the child martyr and the St. Agnes of the Twentieth Century.

Alessandro could not speak. He lowered his head in wonderment. The growing religious importance of Marietta, his victim, the pope glorifying the girl whom he had killed, impressed him beyond words. His crime, her death and burial, and his trial and subsequent punishment, instead of concluding the peasant tragedy of the marshes, surely seemed to be the opening to a great, mystical reality exceeding any of the stories he had read.

He was transferred to the warehouse, unpacking, sorting, marking, and stowing prison supplies. The years began to go by with charitable speed. The prison was his only home, and he adjusted sensibly to its ways. Events brewed outside of the prison of Noto that in sane comparison made life there seem almost preferable to the hazards of freedom. 1912 saw the Italian armies battling in Libya. Fifty Arab war prisoners were brought to the Noto prison. With their desert wear, oriental eating habits, and chanting of the Koran, they provided bizarre color and contrast to the prison. In 1915, Italy entered the World War. Europe in flames and millions of human beings dying, and its aftermath of disease and suffering, did not change or even touch Alessandro behind the sunbaked prison walls of Sicily's isolated Noto.

In 1917, he earned the red ribbon to wear on his sleeve, indicating that he had served the fifteen-year half of his sentence. The earth toil, the field labor he had been incensed about as a youth in Le Ferriere, his arms now longed and ached for. He was none other than a peasant, a son of the soil. All he wanted now was to wrestle the earth. He made an application to the warden for transfer to an agricultural prison colony in Sardinia. But transportation of prisoners had to be deferred until after the war. In the meantime, the sympathetic warden permitted him to leave Noto behind and join the prison camp above Siracusa in the mountains of Augusta, where the change of environment and the arduous work of cutting and transporting stone down to the seaport was to his liking.

During 1918, he received the letter from his sister-in-law Maria, Pietro's wife, informing him that his father Giovanni had died in the poorhouse of Ancona. His father was taken away by death from lifelong misery. Alessandro wept and prayed for the father he had failed and disgraced sixteen years before in Le Ferriere. But that certain defensive reasoning within his blood said, "I did kneel to a son's duty and was his silent staff. Never did I cause him distress until the evil moment gathered me. Why did it have to be me!" And with the passing of his father, he felt close to him for the first time.

The World War was over. To Alessandro, the reported devastation and mass slaughter seemed a fantasy of journalism. As a free man, he might have been killed or disabled during the war, but by a circumstance of the law, he had been sheltered, fed, clothed, and especially protected from the horrendous dangers. He could not help but reflect upon this paradox of life and experience the satisfaction peculiar to the fact.

During Holy Week, 1919, he was among the group sent to Sardinia. Despite the discomfort of the hard, iron handcuffs and the unavoidable humiliation of being gazed at by curious passengers, the lengthy trip by train up along the Mediterranean coast to Livorno, and the sea voyage to Porto Torres, Sardinia, was a memorable and happy interlude.

The penal colony of Bitti was atop a rugged plateau three thousand feet above the sea. Year in and year out, he bore with the patience of his continuously strengthening faith and prayer the harsh life of the Sardinian wilderness.

The life in Sardinia was consonant with his peasant roots and nature; it was the return to the soil, the communion with that which feeds and sustains men, the docile domestic beasts, and the good, fruitful earth. In the winter there was the cutting down of the forest; with spring came the ploughing behind great, white oxen, the sowing of the grain, the tending of the vineyards, and the planting of new vine shoots, working the vegetable garden, the milking of the cows and goats, the shearing of the sheep, the reaping of the wheat with sickles, the threshing of the wheat under the trampling hooves of the oxen, the harvesting of grapes, and the making of wine. At night his healthy, tired flesh rested while books made him forget he was Alessandro Serenelli and took his mind to behold other lives and fates.

There was no chaplain or regular religious services, but on Christmas and Easter, a missionary priest came to the colony and celebrated Mass. During Holy Week, he and the other convicts were escorted by the armed guards up the mountainside to partake of spit-roast lambs, herbs, cheese, bread, and wine with the Sardinian shepherds.

At the Bitti colony, except for a sympathetic acquaintance with a Roman convict named Gabriele Alfanso, he stayed apart from other convicts and did not care for the involved ties of friendship. On winter nights, when not reading, he would listen at length to Gabriele's tales of his adventurous past. Gabriele had deserted the army, robbed his way around the world, was captured and imprisoned in Messina; during the earthquake, he escaped from the shattered prison and resumed his career as an outlaw; finally he was traced to France by the police and returned to prison.

~ 7 ~

1929 WAS THE year that again changed Alessandro's life. One day in January, while he was feeding the chickens and gathering eggs, a guard brought him startling news. The king's son, the Prince of Piedmont, on the occasion of his forthcoming wedding, had granted a measure of amnesty to long-term prisoners with good conduct records, and he was among those who were soon to be released from prison. He immediately sent a letter to his brother Pietro and knelt in prayers for hours, certain that it was Marietta who was opening wide the prison doors for him.

March 11 was the day he had desired for twenty-seven years. He put on the new suit Pietro had sent him. It was unbelievable that he had shed the striped wool convict's garb.

The remaining convicts were glad for him and wished him well. Gabriele clapped him on the back and exclaimed, "Serenelli, with your new suit you leave the hell of prison looking every bit like an important man of the world!"

As he got into the cart headed for the port of embarkation, they called out, "Alessandro, God be with you!" He nodded and waved farewell.

Aboard the steamer from Olbia to the mainland port of Civitavecchia, the carabiniere escort unlocked his handcuffs and fraternized with him.

"Serenelli, how does imminent liberty seem to you after twenty-seven years of prison?"

Gazing over the spacious, green sea, Alessandro shook his head and sighed. "Liberty seems to me a sort of chimera, a word that was never meant for me. The phenomena of liberty I ragingly wanted as an inexperienced youth, even as one who unreasonably yearns for nonexistent castles in the sky. Now, grateful as I am that it is God's will for me to be free, liberty seems a fearful height in space that dizzies me."

"If I were you, brother, I would make up for lost living and not fill my head with airy stuff. I would leave philosophy to professors and the security of Heaven to the priests, and without ado get me a solid young woman and a patch of land. Books belong in school, the religious in church, and the peasant on the land. As you should know, there is considerable propaganda afoot to make Maria Goretti a saint. That is no small thing, and an insupportable situation for one who has already paid the best years of his life for her death. You will be expected to walk the edge of the razor. If I were you, I would migrate and change my identity."

He was taken to the Regina Coeli prison in Rome for the processing for release. It was the same labyrinthine beehive smelling of detained men, the same scenes of chambers, cells, guards, carabinieri, lawyers, clerks, and the confused newly jailed to which he was shunted in fetters twenty-seven years before. It seemed centuries, other lives ago, and yet it was as though yesterday, like a story he read before falling asleep in his cell of Regina Coeli. He had been drawn into a trapping and suffocating dream, and suddenly by a stroke of sorcery awoke at the age of forty-seven. All along he had had a dread of dying in prison, like a bird who hoped only to die beyond the bars of his cage. Since the amazing dream-vision of Marietta in the Noto prison, he felt there was an unusual destiny for him to fulfill. Just what it was, he could not clearly define. Whatever it was had to take place within the gate of penance. This he knew. But hidden deep in the well of his being, there was still the sense of creatureliness that would acridly always question why it was he who had to be frustrated into the sensuality that invited murder, infamy, and the condemnation of most of his life to prison. Why did it have to happen to Alessandro Serenelli!

On March 18, accompanied by a carabiniere and still handcuffed, he was taken to the huge railroad station of Rome for the trip to Ancona and his hometown of Torrette. Awaiting the train, he saw himself in a full-length mirror. The last time he had seen and gone past that mirror was the Sunday afternoon, July 6, 1902. Then, his long dark hair was shining and tousled, his face had been hardly bearded, and rosy with the fullness and bloom of youth, and his mind had been a careless, sullen fort.

Now, he saw a lean man with short-cropped, balding grey hair, bearing a sensitive, knowing, and chastened expression. That he had lived through twenty-seven years of imprisonment and was being set free, to him was none other than a miracle. And he reasoned that it was Marietta's spirit that brought it to pass. Who else?

On the train, the carabiniere handed him a copy of *The People*.[18] "Because of your release, the story of you and Maria Goretti is featured in all newspapers and told over the radio.

As a boy, I read of your crime. My wife and daughters are devoted to the Goretti girl. And here I am taking you to freedom and your hometown. The strangeness of life!"

Reading about himself was hypnotic. The article was a sensational weave of fact and fiction. His father was portrayed as a heartless drunkard and he as the sex-maddened beast of the marshes who, failing to rape a little peasant girl, stabbed her twenty times with a long, sharpened file, and after having left her for dead, returned to deal her ten more piercing thrusts. The Alessandro Serenelli he was reading about was purported to be violently anti-social and a rapist and killer by nature until Maria Goretti's spirit came to him in his cell and transformed him into a peaceful penitent, who might possibly, in gratitude for the miraculous change wrought in him by this saint-like victim, seek to end his days on the path of holiness.

Under the heading "Dawn of Glory," the article related a recent event in the popularly growing religious efforts to elevate further the memory and significance of Maria Goretti:

> The years had passed since the little heroine was martyred in preserving her virginal purity, and the time had come to observe the rule of the Nettuno cemetery to exhume the dead and the removal forthwith the corpses' remains to the common but consecrated bone-heap.
>
> All were in concord that the remains of the dear young girl were not to be dispersed to the indiscriminate community bone-heap, but there was difference of opinion as to the location of the new sepulcher. The archpriest Don Marinelli

of Corinaldo wanted her birthplace of Corinaldo honored with her final resting place, but the Passionist Fathers instead wanted her to rest in Nettuno, in the area of the scene of her martyrdom, and already had a sanctuary prepared for her in the newly reconstructed Our Lady of Graces Church. Assunta Goretti was content to donate to the Passionists for permanent sanctuary in the Our Lady of Graces Church the remains of her beloved daughter. The good mother Assunta, accompanied by her son Mariano and the inseparable and faithful Teresa Cimarelli, was present at the disinterment of her child. The moment of exhumation was most dolorous for the poor mother. Her beautiful and angelic flower was naught but a skeleton. Sustained by a mysterious power, she quietly contemplated the various bones. Then she cried out, "If only my tears could reanimate these white bones of my Marietta!" And tenderly taking the skull of her child from the casket, she pressed it to her breast and kissed at long last again the brow of her Marietta.

Today the killer of Maria Goretti has completed his debt to society. Will he remember that she said, "Alessandro, I forgive you ... I want your soul with me in Paradise?" We hope he does, and that the penitent killer, Alessandro Serenelli, will ultimately find the peace the blessed child Maria Goretti wanted for him.

The carabiniere said, "Serenelli, could you ever have imagined that a celebrated cause would result from the one bad thing you did in all your life?"

Alessandro solemnly shook his head. As though talking to himself he said, "Too much, it is all too much for me. I return as a Lazarus who wishes to be forgotten. The sin I committed has equally ripped Assunta's heart and my own. But why does the newspaper mix the wheat of truth with the chaff of fiction? They have slandered the memory of my poor father, whom destiny bedeviled to the very end. And the weapon I used was not a long, sharpened file. And again, after my momentary madness had spent itself, I locked myself in my room and did not return to finish Marietta!"

After two days of questioning and probationary instructions at Ancona, the hour of actual liberation came. He was to remain with his brother, Pietro, in Torrette and be under special police vigilance for a year, during which time he was not to be seen out of doors earlier than 5:00 a.m. or later than 8:00 p.m., nor walk obscure bypaths, assemble with more than two other persons, nor frequent public places such as shops, taverns, the cinema, and churches. The final words of the marshal had been, "Serenelli, you will do well to always remember that you are known and on record as an attempted rapist and convicted murderer. Woe to you if you again transgress the law!"

He listened obediently to the marshal's parting, drastic warning. The marshal relented, smiled, and said kindly, "Serenelli, the rest of your life is yours now. You are no longer a youth. Use the remaining days God allows you like a decent, sensible Christian man, and all should go fairly well with you." He clasped Alessandro's hand and nodded to his attendant carabiniere. The carabiniere silently led him out into the sunlit street.

Church bells were ringing for the morning Mass. He was no longer an imprisoned convict. He was no longer a number. He, Alessandro Serenelli, was a free man. He left like one who has just come out from under the crisis of a long, seemingly incurable, and near fatal illness. As he walked the few miles along the Adriatic coast road to Torrette, there was a levitation to his being. He had made it—yes, he had made it—he had safely negotiated to the end the many hard years imposed upon him. Human nature, finite and derivative, wanted him to laugh bitterly within.

~ 8 ~

Torrette had changed: everything seemed new, sights he had never seen, different houses, factories, a busy and fast-moving maze of electric trolleys, automobiles, bicycles, and motor scooters. He was lost and wandering in a mechanical world. By the village fountain, he recognized an aged peasant and asked him the direction to his brother Pietro's house.

After informing him, the old man said, "If you had not told me, I would not have known who you were, but I certainly remember you as a little boy, and later I heard of your misfortune. The news of your release is much known. Look about you. The girls of today are painted, smoke cigarettes, wear immodest dress, and gaze boldly into your face. When you and I were young, not even the gypsy women in the carnival behaved as brazenly.

"Today one does not have to rape or kill: there is no need to, for it is the female now who seduces the male. I am not overly religious, but I ask, does God want it this way? And if the Church chooses to claim that the Goretti girl is a saint, will she, as a symbol, be able to turn bad girls into good? No, I do not believe so; the simple, moral, old days are gone, and virtue has gone out of style.

"Anyway, my son, it is as rare as a miracle to see you again, and as though you have returned from the dead."

He stood at the door of Pietro's house. He had left that house when he was sixteen with unformed dreams in his heart, and come back as an ex-convict of forty-seven, scourged by life. The door opened. Neither he nor his brother recognized each other. After the strange moment of identification, they embraced and wept. That night, with Pietro's wife and grown children, there was the feasting of the poor and rejoined. It was the first bread and wine partaken in freedom since the lunch Marietta had prepared for him on the day he attacked her.

He did not want to talk about his prison years. The new, Fascist order of government, technical progress, and what was going on in the world were all distant and unfamiliar things to him. It was difficult in the following days to make conversation with his nieces and nephews. What had he to do with the activities of the world that had long since gone past him? The never-ceasing social streams of life had left him behind, as a lost island, the hour Marietta died. There was only one person who belonged with him to that day: Assunta Goretti. World upheavals and changing times could not alter that tragic bond.

Three miles away and visible from Torrette was the hill city of Corinaldo, where Assunta lived with her daughter Ersilia. Each day he wanted to go to her but did not have the courage to do so.

During the year of his probation, Pietro found odd jobs for him. When the period of police surveillance was over, Pietro said, "Now that the law has finished picking the flesh from your tail, why not settle to a normal life with a woman. The widow Valeria, not concerned about the furor of the past or the religious importance of the Goretti girl, needs a son-in-law on her land and has made to me the practical proposal that you marry her daughter, Elena. And why not? As for the world, it will talk about you but not give you bread. Take Valeria's daughter, and you will be systematized with land to work, a roof over your head, and a young, robust wife in bed. Say the word and I will arrange it."

Alessandro shook his head.

"I am grateful to Valeria and her daughter, but my proper thoughts dwell not on marriage. Marriage in the beginning would seem beautiful, but then would come sorrow as my children would have to grow under the stigma of a father who had been a murderer and convict. Believe me, dear brother, when I tell you a bitter life has put out the fires of my youth, and twenty-seven years of imprisonment has made loneliness my only possible home."

With permission from the police department to seek work as a farm hand, he left Pietro's house and the village of Torrette.

Then began his directionless wanderings for subsistence among the callous migrant field hands from one remote village and agricultural holding to another, hoeing and ploughing a few days here and sowing, weeding, cultivating, reaping, and threshing there. The ignorant peasants did not know who he was. But wherever he went, all soon noticed how unlike themselves he was. He never complained, blasphemed, or gave way to rage; he was the first in the field and the last to leave, scrupulously obeying orders and sweatily toiling in silence. Sooner or later, the curious would find out he was the Alessandro Serenelli who had killed the little girl whom the Church was intending for sainthood, and from the resulting superstition, and fear of him, those about him forced him to leave and move on. New employers, on learning his identity and fearful that he might compulsively revert to a crime of lust, watched him warily and relegated him to sleep in the barn or stable. Freedom brought him insecure and doubtful bread, defenseless exposure to unjust suspicion, and occasions that threatened to make of his life a complete and irreparable disaster.

An elderly sharecropper, who valued his strength in the field and his quiet manner, told him, "Serenelli, I know your story, and it does not interest me in the least. As long as you work hard and behave, I consider you a part of my family." But the florid, young wife of the sharecropper became desirous of him. One day, while sickling grain by his side, she offered herself. He backed away in consternation. Repelled, she asked mockingly, "You killed a girl for the very same thing I freely offer you. Have you become holy since then, and do you fear a woman?"

"In all respect to you, please believe me," he answered softly, "that when one has been bitten by a serpent, he fears even a lizard."

The young peasant woman shrugged with pity for him.

After the harvest and threshing, he asked the kind, old farmer for his wages and left without explanation.

It was not the same world he had left behind in 1902. During his detention, the mass sufferings and convulsions of the great World War and its wake of fascism generated a licentiousness throughout the land that did not leave the peasantry untouched. It was only the grimness of poverty that had stayed the same.

The people of the land seemed to be struggling between good and vast evil.

Wherever he found work as a farmhand, the mark of his past soon found him, and either an infatuated woman sought him as husband or lover, or his employer, not wishing the embarrassment caused by his notoriety, sent him away. He longed only to again see Assunta Goretti and to open his heart to her. The freedom he had waited twenty-seven years for was a cold, unfeeling, disturbing vacuum in which he felt homeless and naked. He who had in a self-goaded, distorting heat of youth clamored for destroying expression, now had a reverence for the sacredness of all life and was sensitive to and saddened by even the shadow of a violent hand or voice. When his fellow-farmhands drank and fought and bawdily proclaimed their sexual exploits, he shrank. He was timid within the freedom of a world that was not free of its willfully sinful self. He wanted peace and to find his soul, and he prayed to her who as a child had assured him of the safekeeping of his soul.

~ 9 ~

THE WEEK BEFORE Christmas 1934, while he was working on a farm in the region of Osimo, Alessandro received a surprising letter. It was from old Don Francesco Bernacchio, the archpriest of Corinaldo, inviting him there for the Christmas holidays. The priest also enclosed trainfare for Alessandro.

Alessandro arrived at the rectory of Our Lady of Sorrows Church in Corinaldo early Christmas Eve. He hesitated at the entrance as a trembling came over him that he could not understand. As he knocked on the door, the bell in the tower tolled, and from within the lighted church voices were raised, singing, "Peace on earth, to men of good will." A serving woman opened the door. Behind her, smiling, was the archpriest.

"What is it, Assunta," asked Don Bernacchio.

"A man," the woman said.

Alessandro's vision misted. This white-haired woman in black was Assunta Goretti. He had last seen her on the day he was sentenced to prison — thirty-one years before.

"Do you recognize me?" he asked her.

"Yes, my son," responded Assunta tearfully.

He threw himself at her feet and cried, "Do you forgive me, Assunta? Dear Assunta, forgive me, forgive what I have done to Marietta and you!"

Assunta placed her hands upon his head, caressed his face and said, "Alessandro, Marietta forgave you, Christ has forgiven you, and why should not I also forgive? I forgive you, of course, my son."

He arose, and they embraced.

"Alessandro," she said, "throughout the long years, I have prayed to Marietta for you. I have expected you since you left prison. Why have I not seen you sooner? Your evil days are past, and to me you are as a long-suffering son."

Assunta led Alessandro to Ersilia's house nearby. On the way, they paused before the large, white marble statue of Marietta that the people of Corinaldo had erected. Alessandro removed his cap and timidly kissed the feet of the statue and let his tears fall upon the pure white stone.

That night, on the third floor of number 34 on the Via Borgo Mazzini, where Assunta lived with her daughter, Ersilia, there was a scene of great Christian rejoicing. Assunta had taken Alessandro into the small dining room off the kitchen. Present were Ersilia, whom Alessandro had last seen as a child of four; Teresina, who had been a baby asleep by Marietta as she was repairing the shirt on that fatal morning so long ago; Mariano, who at nine had seen Marietta's bloodied form minutes later and ran in fright, and Ersilia's husband, Euliano, and their three growing children. Teresina was now Sr. Maria Alessandro of the Franciscan missionaries.

Assunta said, "The Infant Jesus has tonight brought Alessandro to our midst." They nodded, and one by one gave Alessandro the traditional welcoming embrace and kiss upon both cheeks. Assunta's charitable love that night was unmixed and direct. From her hands Alessandro received the bread and fish and wine celebrating the birth of Christ. His heart was full. This was the fullness of the message of virtuous love that the child Marietta had known by grace.

It had been thirty-one years since Assunta and Alessandro had broken bread together, and there was much to be told. The Cimarellis appeared, and Teresa Cimarelli, who also had moved back to Corinaldo, greeted him warmly.

"Alessandro, finally! You are thin but look in good health. Son, tell us, for we are Christians together, how was the cross of prison?"

"Godmother Teresa," Assunta said gently, "it would be best not to remind Alessandro of the many painful years."

But Alessandro answered, "The first six years in prison, I was void of spirit and my mind was a turbulence of desperate and violent thoughts. It was following the Messina earthquake that Marietta appeared to me in a dream. From that time, my despair gave way to resignation, and I began to enjoy a feeling of serenity. As for all the prison years—they are hard memories to be forgotten."

Assunta told of her incessant struggle to raise her children, and of how God and Marietta provided strength.

She had begged alms and worked in fields and homes, she said. Pope Leo had sent money for the education of Ersilia and Teresina. As for Angelo and Sandrino, they were not content to remain peasants and wanted to better their lot. One night, Angelo dreamed of Marietta, who said, "Go to America. There is money to be made there."

"I did not have a cent to give him," Assunta recalled, "but like a miracle, a friend loaned him the fare to America.

Sandrino went to America later. I never saw him again, for he died there in 1918."

It was only by a miracle from Marietta that Mariano was still alive, Assunta recalled. His battalion was preparing a bayonet assault, and Mariano and the other soldiers were standing in the trench awaiting the signal. The order came. Mariano commended his soul to God and Marietta and invoked their aid and was about to charge out of the trench when a voice called loudly, "Mariano!" He turned and bent to see who called him. In that instant, a German bomb exploded nearby. His companions were blown to little pieces, but Mariano was not so much as scratched.

"No one but his dear sister had called to him at that moment to have him bend down and be saved from sure death," Assunta declared.

And Assunta spoke of Marietta's glory, of the suggestions of the multitudes and of high powers of the Church that she was a saint. "Whose joy could have equaled mine on the day Marietta's bones were transferred to the sanctuary of Our Lady of Graces Passionist Church in Nettuno?"

The urn containing Marietta's body had been carried by six Daughters of Mary, dressed in white, and behind it there was a long train of religious, civil, and military authorities, and young and old. Everywhere there were flowers, arches, candles, inscriptions, and even fireworks!

After the ceremonies, a Passionist, Fr. Mauro dell'Immacolata of the Scala Santa of Rome, had come to see Assunta, she recalled. "Assunta Goretti," he had said, "it is my intention to work for the sanctification of your daughter, who is acclaimed by all as a true martyr, but it is necessary for me to learn from you of her life."

"I told him what I remembered of those days when she graced the earth and of her beautiful virtues. But then I told Fr. Mauro I felt it unseemly for a mother to eulogize her own child."

"No, no, Assunta," he had said. "It is not unseemly for you to talk of your blessed child. You must tell me everything—about the Gorettis and the Serenellis during the time of your daughter's life. Your information will serve me for a work of such scope that you cannot even imagine. I have in mind to do a great thing for your Marietta!"

"If my child becomes a saint," Assunta said to Alessandro then, forgetting her reminiscences for the moment, "I shall never cease to wonder and ask, 'Why upon me has Heaven bestowed this incredible honor and not upon some other mother?'"

She paused for a moment, and then continued, "But what will you do now? Will you marry or will you wander as one without hearth and kin? But God in his goodness will respond for you."

She held out a faded booklet. "I have saved the little copy of the *Christian Doctrine* that you gave to Marietta. It is sacred. Take it with you, for I know she wants you to keep it. It is late. We must sleep and go to Christmas Mass in the morning. Come with me to Mass, Alessandro.

"Ah, Alessandro, my son, the ways of God surpass anything we can possibly dream of."

The next morning, the people of Corinaldo witnessed that which could only happen among the poor of Christ. Assunta

Goretti, with head held high and tears falling, took Alessandro Serenelli by the hand as a mother takes a son, and led him to Mass. At the altar rail, side by side, she and he—he, who had killed her daughter—raised their open mouths to partake of the Flesh and Blood of Jesus.

That Christmas holiday was paradise to Alessandro. On the street he was nodded to with sincere friendliness by many people. The three days he was in Corinaldo, he lived in the rectory with Don Bernacchio and spent the evenings with Assunta and Ersilia's family, to whom he was affectionately known as "Uncle Alessandro."

~ 10 ~

AT THE TIME Alessandro and Assunta were together in Corinaldo, little did they know of an extraordinary discussion taking place in the Vatican, concerning Maria.

Cardinal Salotti, Promoter of the Faith, in private audience with Pope Pius XI, was explaining the enthusiasm of German Catholics who were pleading the Cause of a Bavarian girl brutally murdered in defense of her purity a century before.

"Do you believe, cardinal," asked the pope, "that this was true martyrdom?"

"Certainly, your Holiness, since, according to St. Thomas, one who chooses to die in defense of even a single Christian precept is to be regarded a martyr."[19]

Pius, who as Cardinal Achille Ratti prior to his election to the papacy had visited the shrine of Marietta in Nettuno and learned from the Passionists the details of her death, pondered the cardinal's words. He said, "For that matter, we have Maria Goretti. The heroic little martyr's life and death made an indelible impression upon me and has never left my thoughts. Tell me, cardinal, has anything been done for her Cause?"

"No, your Holiness. It properly devolves upon the Passionists, who are the custodians of the Goretti girl's body. The Passionists have labored much to make known the beautiful virtues of the little girl. Is it imaginable to promulgate a Cause of Maria Goretti?"

Nodding and smiling, Pius XI answered, "Yes, cardinal, without loss of time, and accompanied by God's love and my own benedictions."

The canonical process for the investigation of Maria Goretti's sanctity was initiated during January 1935, with Passionist Padre dell'Immacolata nominated as Postulator of the Cause. The serious ceremony was held in the Nettuno Our Lady of Graces Church amongst thousands of adoring girls and prelates crowded around Marietta's sepulcher.

May 31 of the same year saw the first session of the Informative Process at the bishop's palace in Albano below Rome. Passionist Padre Aurelio had brought Assunta Goretti and Alessandro to Albano.

The splendor of the palace, the dignity, the robes of ecclesiastical rank, the tribunal of cardinals, monsignors, priests, clerks, the carabinieri, and the forbidding aspect of the devil's advocate was a wondrous maze, an exalting and fantastic reality to Assunta and Alessandro. How could their peasant lives understand and encompass this tremendous occurrence? It was the accomplishment of her daughter and his victim from the world beyond!

Before the lengthy interrogations, the postulator, Padre Mauro, instructed the mother and the killer to bring forth truthfully "all that which you knew, both for and against, about God's child and little servant, Marietta."

This was the beginning of their many summonings before the exacting questioners of the Informative and Apostolic Process.

Alessandro was questioned closely and critically by the devil's advocate, the Church's official representative of the cynical reaction to sanctity, whose business it is to raise objections to any candidate for Canonization.

"Was not Maria Goretti, like all little girls, naturally curious about life, secretive, vain, religious for the sake of sanctimonious impression on observers?" he asked.

"Did she not tell little white lies now and then? Wasn't she petulant, disobedient?"

"Wasn't she always seeking favor of grown-ups, conscious that she was a girl and he a handsome young man?"

"Was it not possible that she had cunningly excited his interest and led him on?"

"Why did she not run from him as he stood in the doorway of the kitchen and commanded her to come to him? After he pulled her into the kitchen, was she at first fascinated by temptation before changing her mind and putting up resistance?"

"And did she really cry out as he attacked her, 'Alessandro, it is sin ... I forgive you ... I want your soul with me in Paradise!'—or did he make up those words to mitigate his punishment?"

"Was not his dream of Maria Goretti's appearance to him in prison a crafty fiction to obtain sympathy? Was not his contrition a ruse for the purpose of seeking pity and a strange kind of fame?"

"Was not Maria Goretti no different than many other girls killed by rapists?"

"Wasn't he unduly influenced by the emotionalized versions written about Maria Goretti and the unique sentimental aura created about her by Church and public?"

Alessandro protested all of this, weepingly. In forthright peasant language and with honest words, he retold the story of the days of Le Ferriere, his complete esteem for Maria's goodness, the torment of his frustration, and his mad decision to rape or kill her. He concluded simply, "No insinuation can ever be aimed at Marietta. All the fault and guilt are mine. I willingly let myself be blinded by evil and destroyed Maria Goretti, who was as innocent as water."

Alessandro's testimony during all the proceedings proved to be most potent and precious in the eyes of the Church and to Fr. Mauro's ardent efforts in the Cause of Maria Goretti.

While their Marietta, under the auspices of the great church powers, was now assuredly a saint in the making, Assunta returned to her charwoman labors in Corinaldo, and Alessandro to the grain fields of Osimo. A few months later, he fell gravely ill with pneumonia. Lingering between life and death, he invoked the aid of Marietta, whom he now considered his protectress in Heaven. He wanted to live only for the sake of fulfilling his penitence. And when he passed the crisis of illness, he thanked Marietta for saving him. After two months in the Osimo hospital, he arose from his sickbed a physically broken man.

Again it was Christmas time, and he journeyed to Assunta and Don Bernacchio in Corinaldo. In the rectory of Our Lady of Sorrows, he told his host of his near-fatal illness, and that he wanted to cease his useless wanderings and to root amongst some religious somewhere.

Don Bernacchio replied, "Tomorrow, Christmas, a Capuchin, Fr. Monterado, will arrive. He can open many doors. It seems God wants me to find you refuge in a monastery—and where else would a penitent end his days? In my way, somehow, I shall arrange it. Until then, stay under the shelter of the Lady of Sorrows."

Don Bernacchio kept his word, and in May, the Capuchin monastery of Amandola offered sanctuary to Alessandro. The superior, Fr. Cingoli, received him kindly and assigned him to light all-round tasks in company with a senile domestic named Mugnetto.

It seemed Alessandro's driven wanderings were over. But old Mugnetto, worrying that he might be considered useless and ordered from the security of the monastery in favor of Alessandro, conceived a stratagem for getting rid of Alessandro. He went weepingly to the superior and swore that coincident with Alessandro's arrival his life's savings of 4,000 lire had been stolen from under his mattress.[20] He claimed that as Alessandro shared his room, it could have been none other than he who had searched the bed and took his hoard.

The superior had no other recourse but to notify the marshal of the carabinieri of the theft.

Alessandro was summoned before the superior and the marshal. With humiliation, he had to identify himself. Yes, he was the very same Alessandro Serenelli who had murdered the little Goretti girl and had been in prison with many other criminals for twenty-seven years. When questioned about the alleged theft, he could barely speak and tremblingly denied having known about Mugnetto's savings.

The marshal pitied him, shook his head, and said, "Either Mugnetto has misplaced his money or is lying for some reason of his own. Or you have learned well in the school of prison, could not resist taking the money, and are telling me an untruth to save yourself."

"I know nothing of Mugnetto's money," said Alessandro humbly.

"I must hold you suspect until I find the answer. Do you know where the police station is in the city?"

"No, sir marshal."

The marshal instructed him and commanded, "Go to the police station and present yourself to the jailer for incarceration."

Alessandro nodded obediently. He left the monastery immediately and found his way to the police station.

The jailer was surprised. "You come all by yourself to be jailed? This is new and strange. What crime have you done?"

"None. I have been mistakenly—or wrongly, if you will—accused of a robbery in the monastery of the Capuchins."

The jailer wrote down his name, age, occupation, and background, removed his personal effects from his pockets, and locked him in a cell.

Before he left, he said, "Serenelli, you contend that you are innocent. It is said that where there is smoke there must be fire. If you are not telling the truth and are proven guilty—my man, it would be far better for you to obtain a rope and hang yourself."

He was again oppressed by walls and caged with bars. Day followed day and the bars were still about him. Fears assailed him. Suppose Mugnetto had planted the money among his belongings, in his valise or in his mattress, and upon that he was adjudged and convicted of the theft? Who would regard his protests and his plea for justice? Then he would surely have to end his days in prison—this time for something he did not do—and would there be prison awaiting him in the world to come? No, Maria was there for him. He sent his prayers to her—she knew he had not taken Mugnetto's money.

The morning of the fifteenth day, the marshal came to him. "Cheer up, Serenelli, I have come to release you. From the beginning I sensed you did not touch Mugnetto's money. Old Mugnetto confessed that he tried to frame you. Try to forget it all, you are free."

On his return to the monastery, the superior gave him disheartening news. "Alessandro, I regret to say that this episode casts an unpleasant cloud over your stay here. Hurtful tongues will wag in spite of your innocence. It would be best for you to seek work and sustenance elsewhere. It grieves me, but I must ask you to leave our community."

What would the elsewhere be? How long, for how long would he be a home-seeking Ulysses?[21]

Again he was a refugee of Don Bernacchio in Corinaldo.

"Patience, my son," said Assunta to him as she swept the floor of the rectory. "Marietta will soon find the safe roof for you!"

Two letters arrived offering Alessandro a haven, one from the Passionists of San Marcello and the other from the Capuchins of the not-too-distant Ascoli Piceno. Don Bernacchio counseled him that, in view of the fact the Passionists were sponsoring the Cause of his victim, it would be better as part of delicacy and discretion to settle with the Capuchins.

"Ascoli Piceno," said Assunta, "is nearer here, and you can visit us more often, Alessandro, my son. Do as Don Bernacchio advises and enjoy peace and prayer with the Capuchins."

Don Bernacchio obtained an automobile and driver, and he and Assunta accompanied Alessandro to the city of Ascoli Piceno in the mountainous Abruzzi. They arrived there on the feast day of the patron of Ascoli Piceno, St. Emidio.

The Capuchin monastery, originally built by the Benedictines, was a thousand years old, of Romanesque design, and beautiful. In the garden by the ancient fountain, before she left, Assunta embraced Alessandro.

"Remember, we are the children of God. When first I saw you, a motherless, unloved youth, I took you to my bosom — as a Christian woman, could I have done otherwise? God willed you to be spiritually lost and then the found son of my heart, in spite of the horrid happening of the long past."

Alessandro was now fifty-four. God had pitied him and brought him into the calm sea, and for that his being was filled with gratitude. The monastery was secluded and apart from the world, and the sins of the world could not reach and hurt him there. With his peasant farming experience, he became the monastery gardener, having rich earth to work, perfect orchards to attend, the barnyard beasts to care for, and about him the tame birds, cats, and dogs. The good Capuchins called him brother, and there was the chapel and daily Mass to attend and the peace for prayer and solitude.

~ 11 ~

THEN CAME THE grotesque and raging years of World War II, bringing a continuous maelstrom of death, destruction, and deprivation, with evils so vast, deaths of innocents so numerous, and sufferings so inhuman that tragedy was rendered a meaningless word. The force of war swept through, excoriated, and left in ruins the locales of the Goretti-story: Nettuno, Le Ferriere, Ancona, and Ascoli Piceno.

During the war days, Alessandro, along with the Capuchin Fathers, worked holily, indefatigably to save life and alleviate sufferings in Ascoli Piceno. The First World War had found him protected from its terrors in prison, and the Second World War as an aging man sheltered in a religious community. For this he sincerely attributed his preservation to Marietta. But as for Assunta, the privations of the war, and age, took their toll. In 1944, she was crippled and invalided by a paralytic stroke. Assunta's days of hard toil were over. From then on, she could rest in her chair by the window and look out to the street and the Our Lady of Sorrows Church across the way.

Despite war's demands, dangers, and burdens, Padre Mauro was devoted to the Apostolic Process of Maria Goretti's Cause. By successive stages were completed the *Antipreparatoria* on October 27, 1942, the *Preparatoria* on February 1,

1944, and the *Generale coram Sanctissimo* on January 1, 1945.²² From these studies, it was established that little Maria Goretti had all the character of a true martyr, not dissimilar to Christian martyrs of the early centuries such as Agnes, Cecilia, Lucia, and Agatha.

Subsequently, on March 25, 1945, His Holiness, Pius XII, sent forth the *Decreto* recognizing the martyrdom of Maria Goretti. Then on May 21, following the *Decreto*, he declared that the Church could securely proceed with the rites of her Beatification.

The Beatification though, had to wait until the war had run its ghastly course and peace had returned to the devastated land and the nearly crushed people. The military occupation by enemies and allies alike tended to profane family life and shamefully deprave the moral fiber of the young. As never before, the spirit of Maria Goretti was needed as a virtuous hope and inspiration toward purity for girls in Italy and all lands.

Marietta's Beatification took place on April 27, 1947, the third Sunday after Easter. St. Peter's, the largest Christian temple in the world, could not contain half the people who had journeyed from near and far lands and who joyfully came to pay homage to a poor, little, illiterate peasant girl now being elevated to the glory of the altars.

Assunta Goretti and her children — Mariano and his family, Ersilia and her family, and Teresina (Sr. Maria Alessandra of St. Alfredo) — and the Cimarellis were present. Assunta with her eighty years, white hair, work-gnarled hands, time-ravaged, strong, God-loving face, by the grace of Heaven had lived to witness the blessing of the fruit of her womb. Tears cascaded within Assunta. She had borne a girl who preferred death to sin, a child who saw the soul all-precious and forgave lust-demented Alessandro. Now mankind saw Marietta as she had long ago known her child in the farmhouse of Le Ferriere, as a saint.

After the reading of the *Decreto* declaring the Beatification of Maria Goretti came the *Pontificale* with the solemnity proper to the great occasion. That evening, Pius XII celebrated the Mass venerating the new *Beata*, and Assunta heard the Vicar of Christ sing, "*Ora pro nobis, Beata Maria Goretti!*" and grateful exaltation captured her heart for the value of her good child! Following the Mass to Marietta, His Holiness came to Assunta and embraced her. She clasped and kissed his hands.

His Holiness took her hands to his lips and said with tears of joy, "Assunta Goretti, blessed art thou for having had such a daughter!"

To honor Corinaldo as Marietta's birthplace, the postulator, Padre Mauro, authorized by Cardinal Natucci, Promoter General of the Faith, gave to Assunta Marietta's right arm—the arm with which she sought to defend herself from Alessandro's fury—to be enshrined on the altar in the crypt of the Lady of Sorrows Church.

On the Beatification event, Alessandro wrote to Pietro's family,

> The feast of Marietta's Beatification in Rome was also a profound and festive rejoicing for my penitent soul. Now I am certain of a protectress

in Heaven. After the celebration for Marietta in Corinaldo, I visited Assunta. In the obscurity of a night, alone and secretly, I went down into the crypt of Our Lady of Sorrows and prayed long hours before the beatified relic of Marietta.

The newspapers as usual have not been objective regarding me and have printed false and unfounded accounts. While here in the monastery of Ascoli Piceno, I read that *I* was in Rome. They said I was especially invited to Marietta's Beatification and was there in the Vatican and St. Peter's wearing sacerdotal robes and with the long Capuchin beard — all inventions of newspaper fantasy! But it is not important what they say about me, and perhaps their fanciful exaggerations constitute part of the expiation for me of the awful crime I blindly committed as a youth.

Marietta, now known as the *Beata*, was invoked by the sick and distressed, and many miracles wrought through her intercession were reported. For the requirement of Canonization, the postulator, Padre Mauro, chose two of undisputable evidence: Anna Grossi Musumarra of Rome, gravely ill with pleurisy, given up by doctors as a hopeless case and having already received last rites, was cured with miraculous suddenness on May 4, 1947, after praying to Maria. Guiseppe Cupo of Rome, a poor day laborer with a wife and four children, had his right foot crushed by a falling boulder. The doctors were deciding to amputate the injured foot. The following morning,

May 8, 1947, there was no sign of injury, and his foot was normal enough for him to return to his heavy work.

The truth of the two miracles was attested and sworn to by an impartial commission of eight doctors before the Congregation of Sacred Rites. On December 11, 1949, His Holiness issued the *Decreto* for the Canonization of Maria Goretti and fixed the date for June 25, 1950.

The scene at St. Peter's on June 24, 1950, had no parallel in the annals of the Holy Roman Catholic Church. Never before had a million souls come to St. Peter's all at one time, nor in Catholic history had there ever been present at the ceremony of Canonization the mother of the saint.

People from all lands and from all walks of life arrived in St. Peter's Square to participate in the ultimate triumph of a little peasant girl's virtue. The crowd was so immense that it was decided to perform the beautiful rites of Canonization out in the curved, sloping piazza, before the multitudes that packed the St. Peter's Square and extended far down the broad Via della Conciliazione.

Looking down, aged Assunta saw in the sunlight the High Altar, His Holiness Pius XII, the procession of the *ecclesiasta*, and men in resplendent uniforms, the dignitaries, the flowers, the standards, the kneeling and rising and again kneeling multitudes, and the flocks of soaring doves and the flowers everywhere, and heard the chants and intonations and responses and finally His Holiness proclaiming Maria Goretti as then and forever included in the catalogue of saints. Then the silver and gold trumpets cried jubilantly, and the five hundred churches of Rome rang forth their bells, and the multitudes pointing to her roared, "Blessed is the mother of St. Maria Goretti!"

But Assunta was seeing more than the pomp and glory and acclaim before her. Assunta was seeing Marietta in the farmhouse kitchen of Le Ferriere, cooking, cleaning, sweating, and comforting her mother's aching body after the long, toiled-wracked day of the fields. She was seeing her child lying in pools of blood. She was seeing her in the hospital room and hearing her say, "Mamma, do not worry about me ... take care of my brothers and sisters ... Mamma, where will you sleep tonight? ... Goodnight Mamma, pray and remember that God will provide ..."

~ 12 ~

FOR THE AGED, time passes all too quickly, and now for Assunta and Alessandro, the years, no longer troubled, passed with painless velocity. Alessandro and Assunta were together more often. On his visits to her, he enjoyed waiting upon her, helping Ersilia in the kitchen, baking bread, and cooking for Assunta. And he would sit by her side, and they would talk and laugh and weep and pray. And filled with the warmth of her maternal love, he would go back to the monastery.

In early September 1954, he visited Assunta. She was failing noticeably, but her mind and humor were alert as ever. In their simple, natural way, they always talked of Marietta, for there were continuous reports of *bona fide* miracles since the beautiful day of her Canonization, even beyond Italy—in Ireland, America and India. And Assunta liked to hear how things went with Alessandro at the monastery.

"Oh, dear Assunta, the newspapers should never have revealed to the public my whereabouts. As now the years weigh more heavily upon my shoulders, I am unable to do the farm work and am somewhat officially the monastery porter, answering the doorbell.

"The bell rings. I open the door and am confronted with a sack of the strangest people one can imagine, each having come for a different rhyme and reason. A woman asked me breathlessly, 'Porter, amongst the Capuchins is there a particular Fr. Alessandro Serenelli here who gives indulgences, hears confession, and celebrates the Mass?' I answered, 'He is here but he is far from being a priest.' 'Do you know him? What does he do in the monastery?' 'He does exactly just what I do,' said I. 'He plants cauliflower and artichokes in the garden and so forth.' She went away disappointed. Then there was a man who had travelled a long distance, wanting to beat me with his cane. The understanding Capuchins tolerate these invasions philosophically."

"Oh, my son," chuckled Assunta, "it seems people insist upon making a priest of you—put on the robes, let your beard grow, and have done with it."

It was on that visit that Assunta desired a photograph taken with Alessandro. Ersilia fetched the local photographer. As they were posing, Assunta said, "Am I not your mother, Alessandro? Well then come closer to me."

Before he left Alessandro said, "Assunta, so much has happened, and we have become old."

"Alessandro," responded Assunta, "thanks to God who has generously permitted us to arrive this far!" Then wearily, she said, "I want one more miracle in my life ... and that is for Marietta to come and get me."

One month later, on October 8, while Alessandro was sweeping the chapel, Fr. Valentine came in with a telegram. It was the first telegram he had ever received. His heart seemed about to burst. With shaking hands he opened it. It was from Ersilia with the news that Assunta was dying and had asked for him, to give him her final blessings.

The staunchest of womankind, the mother of forgiveness, the mother like Mary, the only mother for him and his battered life, was leaving him. Fear and weakness overcame him. Without her warmth, commiseration, and encouraging smile, his world would be a field without the sun. He turned to the altar and prayed that Assunta would live yet awhile. Why did he not die before she? Dazedly he went to his room and prepared for the trip to Corinaldo. He implored Marietta, whose picture was on the wall over his bed, for strength to face the loss of Assunta. He felt incapable of motion. He looked into the small shaving mirror. Alessandro Serenelli's life had never been his own; except for one treacherous berserk minute in Le Ferriere, it had been forfeited to the field, prison, and monastery. Alessandro Serenelli had been withheld and shut out from the feasting of freedom, woman, and family that even the least of men exercise and enjoy as a matter of course. Life and the world had rushed past him, and he was a seventy-two-year-old man whose sole belonging was utter submission.

The aged face in the mirror was his; and the thick neck and set jaw said that the salt of doubt and question had never quite left the marrow of his bones. He was as nothing in the permanent dark, except for the two lights that shone upon his heart and vision: Marietta's wounds, that in dream, she brought to him as lilies of Paradise; and Assunta's boundless love that made him her son and Marietta's brother. Assunta was the spiritual air vital to his aged life. In Assunta he had at last seen what Marietta's knew: God's infinite mercy and love. And now he dreaded Assunta's departure from him.

Fr. Valentine came into the room and found him weeping, helpless. He aided him to dress and pack his valise. When he saw Alessandro off at the railroad station, he said, "Peace, brother Alessandro, and gratefully accept what God wills."

Alessandro got to Ersilia's house at nightfall. He climbed the three flights of stairs with anxiety. Ersilia met him in the doorway and embraced him.

"Uncle Alessandro — be Christian strong now... Mamma dearest is dead."

She led him to the bedroom. In the soft light of mutely singing votives, surrounded by Ersilia's family, on the bed with rosary in hand, serene and beautiful in death, was Assunta.

Alessandro cried aloud, "Mamma!" He collapsed upon the bed at Assunta's feet. He kissed her feet and hands and face. And the night long he sobbingly repeated, "Dearest Mamma... Assunta... Mamma, Mamma!"

Assunta had been released from the long, long cross. The fields, poverty, struggle, alms begging, the world's blind blows, the charwoman's day, would command her no more.

Alessandro, with little desire to live on, declined and was physically unable to do work of any sort. The Capuchins retired him to the peaceful and quiet monastery of Macerata. By fortunate coincidence Fr. Valentino was transferred there too.

Each day was now the joy of being treated as an actual Brother Capuchin, filled with hours of reading and devotions. He daydreamed of the normal times in Le Ferriere and saw Marietta come smiling through the fields and calling him.

At night he said his Rosary before the candle-lighted picture of Marietta, praying, "Marietta, I wait for death. Marietta, I await and long for the fulfillment of your promise, your promise that I will be by your side in Paradise, Marietta."

Author's Note
(1962 Edition)

PADRE MAURO RECEIVED me in the rectory of the Passionists' Church of the Scala Santa (Holy Steps) in Rome. Of medium build and with a ruggedly kind face, Padre Mauro is surprisingly young for his eighty years. He does not know the English language; we conversed in Italian. As Postulator of the Cause of Maria Goretti for the Holy See, he had been close to the families and locales of the peasant tragedy, and step by step, throughout many years, he had aided the Apostolic Process to the Veneration, Beatification, and finally the Canonization of Maria Goretti in 1950.

I asked him if the killer of Maria Goretti was alive.

"Alessandro Serenelli," he answered, "is in the Capuchin monastery of Macerata, a mountain town in the region near Abruzzi called the Marches."

We sat, and for hours he retraced for me the lives of the Gorettis and the Serenellis. As dusk descended over the Scala Santa, he invited me into the Chapel of St. Maria Goretti.

On the altar are six large, gold candlesticks and tall, white candles. Glassed-in under the altar is the recumbent figure of the dead Christ, newly removed from the Cross. Above the altar is the oil painting of St. Maria Goretti, and surrounding her portrait are sunbursts of gold. At the altar rail, women and girls were murmuring prayers to her.

St. Maria Goretti is a most beautiful girl in peasant dress, her arms are crossed over her breast, holding the rosary in her left hand and pressing palms and lilies to her with her right hand.

Padre Mauro informed me this is the original portrait from which countless copies have been made and distributed over the world, and that though Maria Goretti had never been photographed in her lifetime, the portrait is her true likeness, painted by a nun from exact description given by Assunta Goretti, her mother.

That evening, Padre Mauro gave me a copy of the small book he wrote containing all the facts of St. Maria Goretti, and also two relics in lockets: a hair of the American saint, Mother Cabrini, and a particle of bone of Maria Goretti.

I visited Padre Mauro before I departed for the places concerned in the story of the Gorettis and the Serenellis.

"My son, do me a favor," asked Padre Mauro. "When you see Alessandro, tender to him my kindest regards and brotherly love. Tell him I often wonder if he still lives, as it has been many months since he has written to me. I wish to know how he is, and how things go with him."

"Suppose the Superior of the Capuchin monastery will not permit me to see him? What if Serenelli does not want to be bothered by me?"

"I will give you two letters on your behalf, one to Alessandro and the other to his Superior; that will help your work. I suggest you first visit Ersilia Goretti in Corinaldo. She will also give you a note to Alessandro.

"I have not seen the saint's sister in some time. Please convey to her my fatherly benedictions. As for Alessandro—if he shrinks from dwelling upon the past, that is his right."

Nettuno is a few hours' drive south of Rome. There, on the strand of the Mediterranean Sea, is the Our Lady of Graces Church of the Passionist Fathers. In a sanctuary to the right, and under an altar, are the visible remains of Maria Goretti. The piazza before the church was crowded with the buses and autos of the pilgrims who had come to pay homage at her shrine.

On the drive inland to Le Ferriere, I passed a farmhouse with a thatched roof. Peasant women were washing clothes in a stone fountain. An old woman and young girls were hoeing in a vineyard. A peasant girl walked by with a bundle of faggots balanced upon her head. Her face was sunburned to the color of the dark reddish earth.

Le Ferriere is easily identified by the high smokestack of an abandoned iron foundry; hence its name "Le Ferriere—the ironworks." There is no village as such; just some dozen buildings old and new, an arched stone bridge over a tired stream, a sharp left turn in the road, and a ten-minute walk to the farm where Maria Goretti lived. There is nothing to indicate the phenomenal fame of the place due to the little peasant girl, only two large, ancient farmhouses set closely at right angles to each other. They are of plastered tufa, two stories, having outside stairways and roofed with red tile.

The Goretti-Serenelli rooms over the barn and stable are open to visitors; the other farmhouse shelters tiny orphans in the care of five Passionist nuns. The few rooms of the Gorettis and Serenellis are divided by the kitchen. The floors are of worn brick, and overhead are the exposed, pitched, time-eaten rafters. In the kitchen there is the fireside, a small altar, and a bronze figure of the felled Maria commemorating the spot where Alessandro had attacked her.

From Rome, it is a nine-hour eastward drive on steep roads up the Apennines and a long serpentine descent from the heights to the hills of Corinaldo, a medieval city above the Adriatic in the Province of Ancona.

Number 34 Via Borgo Mazzini is a centuries-old, three-story, rubble-stone building barely outside the ancient ramparts. On the ground floor is a carpenter shop. I inquired and was told that the elderly woman looking down from a top-floor window was Ersilia Goretti. I called to her and asked if I may come up and speak to her.

"Are you the American writer wanting to know the life of Marietta?"

"Yes."

"I read about you in the newspaper, *Corriere della Sera*. Come up; you are entirely welcome. Watch out for the tight and crooked turns of the stairway."

Ersilia Goretti is a comely, even-featured, smiling woman in her sixties, dressed in black. She is naturally gracious and quite accustomed to being interviewed about the story of the Goretti family. In a glance, I saw that the rooms contained only stark necessities. On a wall of the dining-living room there is a colored lithograph of her sainted sister; beneath it, a shelf holding a votive light, religious articles, a tintype photo of Luigi Goretti in soldier's uniform, and a snapshot of Assunta.

Ersilia presented her husband, Euliano Porfiro, a ruddy-faced, pleasant man. We talked about today and how one lives.

"Euliano," said Ersilia proudly, "was a master mason. But now he is not able to work anymore. We manage though, thanks to God. We have a son in a Vatican post, a married daughter, and a son in the army. A little from here and a little from there, and I do sewing also, which helps." In a corner is a 1918 model Singer sewing machine in perfect mechanical condition.

Euliano put on his beret and excused himself. Ersilia explained, "At this hour the old fellows begin their boccie games by the church school."

I sat at the kitchen table, shelling peas while she trimmed artichokes.

"Ersilia," I said, "permit me to say that you are discarding too many of the good outer leaves."

"I know, but my Euliano does not care for the outer leaves; just the tender parts. The waste does not matter, for I have more than enough artichoke plants in the garden."

While she was doing her cooking over a wood fire in the hearth I said, "Millions of American mothers and daughters revere and pray to your sister."

She nodded.

It is one thing to read about the saints dating from remote times, days of slavery, crucifixions, pagans, alchemy, astrology, gladiators, knights in armor and legends. Now I am in the kitchen of a meager household with a sister of a saint.

Honest bread and wine were blessed. I ate the bread and drank the wine put before me by Ersilia Goretti and felt related to the destiny of the Gorettis. I knew that there was just so much I could learn from the living, and limited Italian biographies about Maria Goretti, and then, that I would have to recreate her story and the aftermath with imagination obedient to the character and spirit of the facts.

I asked Ersilia if she had a scrapbook relative to the wondrous happenings. She humbly nodded her head, rummaged through a table drawer, and showed me some dozen glossy photographs taken at the Vatican during the events of Marietta's Beatification on April 27, 1947, and at the ultimate glory of Canonization on June 25, 1950: Angelo Goretti, who has made the special trip from his home in America, is chatting with a Swiss Guard; Pius XII affectionately receiving white-haired, paralyzed Assunta as Ersilia, Angelo, Mariano, and Teresa, in the habit of a Franciscan nun, look on in incredible awe; and scenes of the vast throngs in the square of St. Peter's attending the ceremonies.

"The pictures in one's heart are of more value than those on paper," explained Ersilia. "But the melody of the poor is to remember worse times. After the woe of Le Ferriere, mother brought us back to Corinaldo. Father at grave's edge with malaria wanted us to return then to Corinaldo—ah, if only we had been able to! Until I married in 1918, following the Great War, we lived uncertainly, working for sharecroppers in the fields and, during the winter, begging alms. With me, Euliano made a home for my mother and brothers and sisters in these very rooms. This house has been in Euliano's family for many generations; thus, roof, by grace of God and goodness of Euliano, we had. Mother was woman-of-all-work for people until she had a stroke when seventy-nine years of age. From then on, the course of her life was from the wheelchair by the window and to her bed.

"Ailing Giovanni Serenelli returned to Torrette and toiled as peasant to his final strength; and, at long last, Alessandro came back to live with his brother Pietro to earn his bread in the fields."

"Did your family feel hate toward Alessandro?"

"My son, what are you saying? Hate is not Christian. After Alessandro finally came to us, he was as one of us. At mother's funeral, he shared our weeping."

Behind Ersilia's house is the Mother of Sorrows Church. Beneath the church is the crypt and chapel of Maria Goretti. Entombed there is Assunta. Enshrined on the canopied altar in a crystal cylinder filled with blue liquid preservative is the age-blackened forearm bone, part of the arm with which Marietta tried to ward off Alessandro's attack. With Ersilia, I lighted candles and prayed before the relic of her sister.

Ersilia showed me Corinaldo's most important monument, in the courtyard of the parochial school, a beautiful, large, pure white marble statue of Marietta. Near the statue is a field, and there in the sunlight I saw Ersilia's husband, Euliano, and a group of old men playing a game of boccie ball.

Ersilia directing me, we drove out of the village to the countryside and the farmhouse where Marietta was born. The farmhouse nestles on a height overlooking a valley beyond which there are waves of hills. Every part of the expanse is meticulously cultivated with vineyards and olive groves. The farmhouse has been there for many hundreds of years; it is small: a ground floor and livestock stall, and a two-room attic above. The walls tell that it was built by peasants: crude, handmade, earthen brick, lumps of tufa, stones of any size, the structure out of square and plumb, tiny windows with rude, wooden lintels, and the lime-clay mortar long since scaling away. There is a marble tablet on the south exterior wall telling the dates of Maria's birth and death and that, though humbly born, the martyr of purity glows on the altar of Heaven in the light of Christ.

In the attic is the little room of her birth, and where the bed was, there is now a white altar. The calcimined walls are inscribed by pilgrims asking for Marietta's protection and heavenly intercession, prayers, expressions of gratitude for favors received, testimonials of afflictions cured and dangers averted. I wrote my name on the panel beneath the altar.

Ersilia and I looked out of the one window upon the halcyon and richly pastorale landscape. She said nostalgically, "Under this roof, father and mother began a family. My family migrated to Le Ferriere for better bread of wheat but harvested the deaths of two most dear. Ah, why, why did they leave from this house, this strip of land?"

Macerata is a three-hour drive southwest of Corinaldo. The road is a winding ascent with sudden turns and descents, and then up again to higher levels with sweeping summits abounding. In the fields, families work the soil with hoes, horned white oxen tug ploughs, men and women prune grapevines, here and there on the slopes a peasant rides a donkey, and shepherds and sheepdogs contemplate their flocks. The land, houses, farmwork, and people are the same as in the days of the Gorettis and Serenellis.

Every village is old, the churches older and many. I stopped in village squares and markets and sounded people out about Maria Goretti and Alessandro Serenelli. They knew that she was the saint of purity, but no one knew about her killer except to conjecture that he might be dead, or a priest, or senile, or insane. No one spoke ill of him; they felt sorry for him and said that a moment of madness could come over anyone, that blind passion happens to everybody, and that there are times variable like the weather in life when it is not humanly possible to resist the devil.

I stood before the entrance of the Capuchin monastery in Macerata. I pulled the bell-chain. A friar came to the door. I explained that I had come from America to do research on the life of St. Maria Goretti and wished to see Alessandro Serenelli. The friar regarded me dubiously. I gave him Padre Mauro's letter. He summoned the superior, who came, accompanied by another friar. I assured the superior that I had not come to embarrass Serenelli in his old age, but wished to treat with him as a fellow Christian.

The superior said, "Aside from our usual duties, we take in from our other monasteries the aged and infirm brothers. This house is their last haven on earth. Fr. Valentino here knows Serenelli very well, having been with him for many years in the monastery of Ascoli Piceno."

I was now in the charge of Fr. Valentino and followed him. He is balding, black-bearded, and about fifty.

We went up to the third floor. The rooms were bare and poor. Fr. Valentino said, "Alessandro is either in his room, on the porch, or in the chapel. He does not work anymore; he is eighty, and recently underwent an operation for the removal of cataracts from his eyes. Throughout the world there is a misconception of Serenelli's status. He is not a monk, but a lay brother of the secular third order."

Fr. Valentino questioned a passing friar who informed him that Serenelli was out on the enclosed porch. We went out onto the porch.

In a corner, standing by a potted lemon tree and gazing out to the vista of mountains and valleys, was a stocky bald man with rosary in hand. Fr. Valentino whispered, "He is Serenelli. I will speak to him, but I cannot promise that he will receive you, nor can I command him to do so."

I could not overhear what Fr. Valentino said to Serenelli. Serenelli did not look toward me. He answered in a low, husky voice and slowly shook his head. I could not blame him. If I were he, I would not want to be at the mercy of authors and the curious. But a host of thoughts and feelings came to me. This is actually he who murdered Maria Goretti. From his crime blossomed a saint who responds to prayers, and through intercession by her miracles happen. The reality of being near her killer was almost beyond comprehension. To the unbeliever, he is only a massive old man, an aged, small giant wearing thick-lensed glasses; to the believer, he is a Christian bearing the cross of his crime, a man indelibly marked as he who destroyed the life of a child-saint.

Fr. Valentino came back to me.

"Serenelli is extremely sensitive about the past. He says it is too painful and indelicate to discuss, and wants it to be forgotten, not remembered and written about. At this time he goes to pray in the chapel. Follow and observe him from a distance. There is no harm in that."

Serenelli wore a brown, coarse wool jacket with a Passionist emblem on the lapel, a checkered flannel shirt, striped wool peasant trousers, and black felt boots with thick felt soles.

I trailed him into the private chapel of the monks. He made the sign of the cross and went to the right end of the front prayer-bench. Standing, he fingered the beads of his rosary with huge hands and softly prayed. Sitting and kneeling behind him on prayer-benches were twelve old monks with long, white beards, some palsied, some hardly able to hold up their heads, all calmly at the brink of the grave. They looked at me for a moment with unquestioning eyes, and then no more.

I confronted Alessandro Serenelli as he left the chapel.

"Signore Serenelli, please listen to me. I bring you messages from Ersilia Goretti and Padre Mauro."

His face lit up.

"Ersilia sends you warmest felicitations, and so does Padre Mauro, who often thinks of you and wonders why your letters to him have ceased."

Tears filled his eyes.

"Dearest Ersilia ... Padre Mauro ... bless them, bless them."

Fr. Valentino and I accompanied him to the refectory, where young monks brought the food to the tottering old. The only adornment in the refectory is a painting of the Last Supper. Fr. Valentino served Alessandro and me a bit of stewed lamb, a bowl of dandelion greens, bread, and a small glass of wine. Serenelli broke the bread with his hands and kissed the bread before biting into it. We ate in silence.

Fr. Valentino walked Alessandro and me out to the monastery garden and left us. Serenelli sensed my sincere desire to be his friend. I told him of my boyhood amongst my people, the immigrant peasants from Abruzzi. Macerata is close to the Abruzzi region. He was compassionately sympathetic about the untimely passing of my parents, and what surprised me and facilitated our rapport was that he had read the Italian edition of my book *Christ in Concrete* and was familiar with the tragedy and struggle of my family.

Having heard my story, he began to tell of his life.

"My mother died when I was a few years old. I never knew her," he sighed. "No one can take the place of a mother. Without a mother's tender care and direction, my life started out on the wrong foot. Then instead of becoming the staff of my father's old age, I gave him the cross of disgrace. Father toiled in the fields until he was seventy-five and died on a poorhouse cot while I was in prison."

He says it is a strange feeling to no longer labor. Without the hoe in his hands, he is conscious of his hands and does not know what to do with them. "The palms of my hands were always calloused as hard as the shell of a tortoise." Now he has all the time for the peace and refreshment of prayer, and the leisure to read books and newspapers, but misses the physical contact of the soil, the hoeing and seeding, the cultivation of vegetables, fruits, and flowers.

I had reached common ground with Alessandro: we were both of Italian peasant blood, are saved and strengthened by the same faith, know manual labor, and relish profound literature.

He bears signs of a once handsome, powerful man: a formidable, well-shaped head and jaw, with even, balanced features; a short, thick neck; tremendous shoulders; a deep chest; and long arms. His wrinkles and brown eyes are magnified by his glasses, his remaining teeth are strong, and the closely cropped hair left about his bald head is silvery-white. His manner is of the solitary, a man who with inspired will achieved gentility, wisdom, and complete victory over flesh and volcanic passion.

"We have an American friar," he said, "a Br. Giles, who is incurably ill. Would you be so kind as to cheer him?"

I went with him to Br. Giles' room. Br. Giles is in his sixties and doomed by emphysema. Br. Giles thanked Alessandro for bringing me to him.

"Good Alessandro was almost right about my nationality; I am a near-American; I am from Newfoundland."

Alessandro was happy for Br. Giles as Br. Giles and I exercised our English language.

"I understand very little Italian," said Br. Giles, "and it does my morale good to speak English."

Br. Giles tells me about his life as a Capuchin in Newfoundland, the British Isles, and Italy. He has a humorous turn of thought and speech. I interpreted his words to Alessandro, and Alessandro beamed.

It was eight o'clock, and Alessandro wished to retire to his room and begin letters to Ersilia and Padre Mauro.

I told Alessandro I was staying in Macerata for a few days and would like to spend many hours with him to learn all I could about the Gorettis and Serenellis. He reflected long and seriously, and then nodded. We shook hands and bade each other a good night.

Fr. Valentino offered me the humble hospitality of the monastery during my stay in Macerata. I sat in the kitchen with him drinking tea and smoking cigarettes. He had been close to Alessandro for twenty-two years in the monastery of Ascoli Piceno and was the only one to whom Alessandro had bared his heart. Fr. Valentino is a man of letters, a rare intelligence. He perceived I meant Alessandro no harm and told me invaluably much about Alessandro's life and character.

In my monastery room, I lay abed thinking about the wonders of faith. The misfortune of Alessandro's life is counterpoised by the forgiveness and intercession of his victim, who guided him to penance and God. If her grace had not reached him, overwhelming darkness would have been his fate. The Catholic Faith elevated Maria Goretti to her whole worth and salvaged the soul of Alessandro.

I awakened, hearing the morning vow recited by the friars in the chapel: "I vow and promise to God Almighty, the Blessed Virgin Mary, our father St. Francis and all the saints, to observe the rule of the Little Brothers, to live in obedience, without property, and in chastity. So be it."

Fr. Valentino led me to Alessandro's tiny room, where Alessandro politely greeted me. There is a cot, a chair, a closet, and desk piled with books and newspapers, and over the cot on the wall, a crucifix and a portrait of St. Maria Goretti.

"Alessandro," I said, "I would like to take you for a drive. We could go to the city and have a morning aperitif, breakfast, and coffee."

Fr. Valentino suggested that he go with me. Alessandro thanked me but firmly declined. Suddenly his face brightened. "My grandniece is being wed today. She and her spouse promised to visit me."

Alessandro and I wandered through the monastery grounds. Young boys wearing black smocks with large, white collars and carrying books coming to the Capuchin school called out, "Good morning, Uncle Alessandro!" He answered happily, "And a blessed good morning to you, my dear boys!"

Some friars were leaving for their daily rounds of alms-seeking; friars were in the kitchen preparing the midday charitable meal for any of the poor and hungry who might present themselves. Friars were tilling the ample vegetable patch, old friars sat somnolently on benches in the flower garden, and Alessandro and I came to rest alongside them. I offered him a cigarette, but he told me he had never acquired the habit of smoking.

During the days I was with Alessandro, he spoke of the past in a barely audible voice. Once, he paused and said, "I remember everything—for what else have I to remember? Yet it all seems to have happened to another person who resembles me and has my name. The revolting crime I committed does not seem real. I have read a thousand books, and somehow the stories all seem more actual than the dark and gloomy events and sufferings of one's own life.

"I always had the desire to learn, to know more and to instruct myself. Even now at the end of my life, with eyes that are of little assistance, I read compulsively. In the time of Le Ferriere, whenever father went to Nettuno, he brought back books and outdated newspapers for me, trying to keep me content. I read and reread everything I could lay hands on; read without much distinction religious books, magazines, journals, educational texts, criminal and horror stories, and romances. Later, they said of me that the walls of my room were covered with lurid and obscene pictures—that is not true—would the government authorities permit such stuff to be publicly sold? I did cut out romantic scenes and figures from newspapers such as *The Messenger* and the *Illustrated Tribune* and paste them on the wall.

"The isolated fret of the marshes would not spare me; it gave me no satisfaction, and I sought to lose and appease myself with reading. During the interminable winter nights, by lamplight I buried myself in reading, as the saying goes, 'just to kill time,' but it seems perhaps that only death kills time. It is to be admitted that the wrong kind of reading influenced my mind and conduct, but as I see it, the prime cause of my ruin was guideless upbringing without a mother. I told you I never saw my mother. I heard my schoolteacher say, 'The greatest tragedy is the loss of a mother.' Being a child, I did not give much weight to these words and simply reasoned that all was well as long as my stomach was filled and there were clothes to cover my skin.

"There were other things within me to reckon with. I was full of health and the exuberance of the lifeforce, being twenty years old. The senses, we know, are like a raging torrent that, if not safely banked, bring death and ruin to the countryside instead of prosperity and riches. In all, though my character was of one timid and apart, inwardly I burned and rebelled acutely against the never-ending harsh labor, poverty, and the savage solitude of the marshes. All this led me to my crime. And for this I have never excused myself.

"Life, though, is never without a 'but.' I told you I had been to sea. My most impressionable years were spent as a mariner, and the habits and life of the sea, like the sea itself, are without moral or remorse, and in my youth, that was to my liking."

He wiped the faded portrait of Maria Goretti with his handkerchief, straightened it, kissed it, and began to describe her.

"Marietta had perfect, regular features, the type of face that at first glance did not particularly attract one's attention;

hers was a plain, quiet, veiled beauty: long chestnut hair, tied at the nape, chestnut eyes, and a healthy, full face. She was robust for her age, but not developed beyond her years as the journalists have represented her to be. She arrived at my shoulders, and I am medium tall. The artists seeking to recreate Marietta have done so by induction and the general likeness of the Goretti family from life, especially her younger sister Ersilia, for in our time photography was rare and the peasantry never dreamed of having their pictures taken.

"Did you know a film was made of the tragedy called *The Sky Over the Marshes*? In my modest estimation, the conception of Marietta that most closely resembled her as she was in life was the young actress, Ines Orsini, who portrayed her. The film was shown to the public in 1949. With permission from the fathers of the monastery, I went in secret to a city where no one knew me and saw the film. I am not capable of judging the art of the story-makers, but in the film version of the tragedy of Le Ferriere, there was much exaggeration, incongruity, falsity, and disservice to the truth. I do not talk about their portrayal of myself, whom they twisted in a thousand ways, but they put the character of my father in a dark light. Poor father! He did not deserve that.

"Story-makers bend the truth to suit their needs. Do two witnesses ever relate an incident exactly the same? Even the Gospels tell each the same story differently. In my humble opinion, God alone knows the real truth.

"They made my father appear heartless, violent, and addicted to wine and vice. But I remember him as a good man. Lawyers were anxious to sue the film people for defamation, but I told them, 'It is not important; perhaps this is part of the expiation of my crime.'

"But as I said before I diverted, the actress in the film, dressed as a peasant girl, most vividly reminded me of Marietta. The day of my crime, Maria wore a colored handkerchief on her head and tied under her chin, and a skirt and blouse of rose tint passed on to her by the Casoni girl who lived near the little Church of St. Antonio."

Days passed, and I learned from Alessandro all he remembered of his act of murder, after-feelings, trial, punishment, the years following his release from prison, and up to the present.

He peered with his failing sight at the yellowed print of St. Maria Goretti.

"Like the rivers running continuously and unerringly to the sea, the sanctity of the girl killed by my hand has spread throughout the world. Even I who destroyed her have given testimony in Rome for the various canonical processes as to the purity and virtue of the martyr—and I did get a proper raking over the coals by him whom they call the devil's advocate. I have heard about the miracles obtained by many people by prayer to her. I know I am not worthy of her help, but yet she is to me in my darkness of sin what the bright and shining star is to the mariner, for her pardon gives me hope.

"I have one desire I wish to realize before my days are closed. Thousands have done something to glorify Marietta, and it would be an injustice if I did not leave behind me something to her memory. I wish somehow to gather together the means to have built here in the monastery a modest chapel and organ to Marietta—the Chapel of Pardon.

"Each night in this tiny room, I put out the light and pray to my saint, my Marietta. I pray, waiting, that the promise the little girl made on her death bed, to receive me in Paradise, will be accomplished; that soon I will leave this mortal flesh and rise to that radiant and serene dawn, where she is, which is the Kingdom of God."

I knelt in prayer with Alessandro Serenelli, and left the monastery.

Endnotes

1. The Pontine Marshes are an area of former marshland in central Italy that includes the small settlement of Le Ferriere. —Ed.
2. Nettuno and Anzio: at the time of this story, two popular seaside vacation towns south of Rome. Both cities were later famous for their significance in the Allied conquest of Italy during World War II. —Ed.
3. Stendhal was the penname of Marie-Henri Beyle (1783–1842), a French realist author. —Ed.
4. Civitavecchia is a major seaport city about thirty-seven miles northwest of Rome. —Ed.
5. These quotations are of unknown origin, but they showcase the philosophical shift of the late nineteenth century away from a Christian or theist anthropology and toward atheism and nihilism. —Ed.
6. The carabinieri (singular "carabiniere") are Italian national armed forces who carry out both domestic and foreign police duties. —Ed.
7. "Death, but not sin!" —a famous resolution of the child-saint Dominic Savio (1842–1857). —Ed.
8. Matthew 8:20. —Ed.
9. See Luke 23:39–43. —Ed.
10. According to the Bible, Jesus died at three o'clock in the afternoon (see Matthew 27:46; Luke 23:44; Mark 15:34). —Ed.
11. The Corte d'Assise (in English, Court of Assizes) is an Italian court that tries serious crimes. —Ed.
12. Capital punishment (also known as the death penalty) is not mentioned by Canalintas or by anyone else because it was banned in Italy in 1889. —Ed.
13. Someone from the Piedmont region in northwest Italy. —Ed.
14. Asia: here referring to Asia Minor, or Anatolia, the peninsula that makes up most of modern Turkey. Saracen: a term for Arab Muslims and their culture. Byzantine: referring to the Eastern, or Greek, Roman Empire in modern Greece and Turkey. —Ed.

15 The source for these quotations is unknown. "The wolf of Rome": according to legend, the founding brothers of Rome were nursed to health by a she-wolf as infants. "The Blessed House of Loreto": the Basilica della Santa Casa, a Marian shrine in Loreto, Italy, which holds a house that many believe was where the archangel Gabriel visited the Virgin Mary. — Ed.
16 Someone from the region of Abruzzo in central Italy. — Ed.
17 Dostoevsky's *Crime and Punishment* (1866) tells the story of a young man, Rodion Raskolnikov, who premeditates and then carries out a gruesome murder. Most of the book focuses on the effects of his actions and the potential punishments he must face. — Ed.
18 *Il Popolo d'Italia*, "The People of Italy": an Italian newspaper founded by Benito Mussolini in 1914 to promote pro-war propaganda during World War I; later it served as the main newspaper of the Fascist movement in Italy until it ceased publication in 1943. — Ed.
19 See St. Thomas Aquinas, *Summa Theologica* II-II, q. 124, art. 5. — Ed.
20 Lira (plural "lire"): Italian currency from 1861–2002. — Ed.
21 Ulysses: Odysseus, famed Greek hero of the Trojan War who was lost for ten years before finally returning home. — Ed.
22 The three formal meetings investigating the authenticity of miracles attributed to the saint. The first two (ante-preparatory, preparatory) are made by a select group of cardinals, and the third (general) under the added presidency of the Pope in the presence of the Blessed Sacrament (*coram Sanctissimo*). — Ed.

Discussion Questions

1. How does the story of Alessandro Serenelli balance the virtues of justice and mercy? How does his life story, especially his repentance and conversion of spirit, show the importance of both?

2. How did you react when you read the author's note at the end of the book and realized that this whole book was influenced by the memories of Alessandro and Maria's sister Ersilia? What do you think of the real Alessandro in the monastery?

3. Which was more difficult for you to read about: the set-up of Alessandro's attack, especially his thoughts and feelings leading up to it in sharp contrast to Maria's chaste character; or the actual attack? Discuss your thoughts and why you felt this way.

4. How did you feel about Alessandro at the beginning of the book? Do you feel that the author over-sympathizes with him; why or why not? What do you think of his dream of Marietta while in prison, his conversion of heart, and the change in his character? How do you feel about him at the end of the book?

5. Think back to Maria's death scene in part 1, chapter 8, or read it again. How does Maria's death clearly parallel Jesus'?

6. The Church names St. Maria Goretti as a martyr. How is she a martyr? Do you agree or disagree with this classification; why or why not?

7. How does Maria's mother, Assunta, respond to Alessandro, to Maria, to doctors, to the court, and to others after the crime? How do you feel about her reaction in the court after Alessandro is sentenced and her actions and responses thirty-one years later when they reunite? What do you think of Assunta, and why?

8. Think back to Alessandro's lawyer's defense speech in part 2, chapter 2, or reread it. Do you agree at all with his lawyer's argument that our culture and society influences people to such an extent as to commit such atrocious crimes as rape and murder? How do you feel about his statement that he is arguing for Alessandro's "truth"? Where do you draw the line as to culture's influence over a person's free will?

9. While he is in prison, Alessandro reflects on the influence reading books has had on his life. We read, "It was ironic that the compelling reading habit that fanned the fire toward his crime in the Le Ferriere farmhouse, now was a wall of solace and his intimate and richly rewarding friend. He realized the fact that the printed word could be a potent influence for the activation of either good or evil. It was like a substance taken into

one's being; putrid air or poisonous food made for illness and even death; the consummation of profound and humanistic letters evoked healthy, compassionate feelings for life." What do you think of his reflection? Do you agree that media such as books or television can have such power over us, or is our will more powerful than their suggestion, and why? What books, or other examples of media, do you feel are good examples to back up your assessment?

10. The theme of liberty and freedom comes up frequently in this book. First, Alessandro wishes to be free from the life of a peasant and is fascinated by the licentious "liberty" of the sailors he once knew. Later, when he is released from prison, he is free from jail, but he not only finds himself still constrained but also reflects upon "the freedom of a world that was not free of its willfully sinful self." How did you see the theme of liberty play out in this book? How does the author's, and Alessandro's, view of liberty compare to that of Pope St. John Paul II, who famously said, "Freedom consists not in doing what we like, but in having the right to do what we ought" (Homily, October 8, 1995)? Who is free in this book, when do they become free, and why? How do they use their freedom?

11. St. Maria Goretti is recognized as a patron saint of chastity and forgiveness. Discuss how she is a model of these virtues.

12. How can St. Maria Goretti, who died rather than be raped, be a comforting patron to victims of rape, both

male and female? Is she an appropriate patron for these souls; why or why not?

13. Sadly, most people today either personally know a victim of sexual assault, or perhaps you are a victim yourself. How can this book, and the story of Maria Goretti, provide healing for victims and their families?

14. "True crime" books, documentaries, and podcasts have seemed to grow significantly in popularity in recent years. In what ways does *I Killed Maria Goretti* fit into the "true crime" genre, and in what ways does it supersede the genre?

15. Reflect on the two Bible passages quoted on the first pages of Part One and Part Two. For Part One, "The Crime," we read from Galatians 5:17: "For the flesh lusteth against the spirit, and the spirit against the flesh. These are at enmity one with another." For Part Two, "Repentance," we read from 2 Corinthians 7:10: "For the grief that is according to God worketh repentance without regret, unto salvation." Why did the author choose these two verses? How do they set up and summarize the two parts of the book?

About the Author

PIETRO DI DONATO (1911–1992) was an acclaimed American writer and bricklayer, best known for his novel *Christ in Concrete*. Born of Italian immigrants in New Jersey, Di Donato left school at twelve to support his family after his father's tragic death. Despite limited formal education, his literary talent flourished. This and his other major work, *Three Circles of Light*, reflect his immigrant heritage and deep humanism, leaving a lasting legacy in American literature.

Sophia Institute

Sophia Institute is a nonprofit institution that seeks to nurture the spiritual, moral, and cultural life of souls and to spread the gospel of Christ in conformity with the authentic teachings of the Roman Catholic Church.

Sophia Institute Press fulfills this mission by offering translations, reprints, and new publications that afford readers a rich source of the enduring wisdom of mankind.

Sophia Institute also operates the popular online resource CatholicExchange.com. *Catholic Exchange* provides world news from a Catholic perspective as well as daily devotionals and articles that will help readers to grow in holiness and live a life consistent with the teachings of the Church.

In 2013, Sophia Institute launched Sophia Institute for Teachers to renew and rebuild Catholic culture through service to Catholic education. With the goal of nurturing the spiritual, moral, and cultural life of souls, and an abiding respect for the role and work of teachers, we strive to provide materials and programs that are at once enlightening to the mind and ennobling to the heart; faithful and complete, as well as useful and practical.

Sophia Institute gratefully recognizes the Solidarity Association for preserving and encouraging the growth of our apostolate over the course of many years. Without their generous and timely support, this book would not be in your hands.

www.SophiaInstitute.com
www.CatholicExchange.com
www.SophiaTeachers.org

Sophia Institute Press is a registered trademark of Sophia Institute.
Sophia Institute is a tax-exempt institution as defined by the Internal Revenue Code, Section 501(c)(3). Tax ID 22-2548708.